The Police State

To

MY WIFE *and* SON

THE POLICE STATE

What You Want to Know
About the Soviet Union

by

Craig Thompson

E. P. DUTTON & COMPANY, INC.
NEW YORK, 1950

30621

Table of Contents

Introduction

WHEN I left Moscow, I smuggled past the censors fourteen pounds of notes which I anticipated would one day form the substance of a book. Altogether, the bundle represented two years of life and work in Russia as a correspondent. It contained scribbled reminders of personal experiences, a tediously compiled who's who of Soviet personalities, stacks of Soviet newspaper items, and a full collection of my dispatches to *Time* and *Life* magazines which had been mutilated or killed by the censorship.

Few countries, except those dominated by the Communist party, would have considered my notes contraband. Yet, in the Soviet Union, my act will be regarded as a crime and this statement of it as my confession of guilt. Such is the gap between us that, had I not tried to smuggle out my notes, I would have been, in my own eyes, guilty of a more reprehensible sin against my profession. My job, as I view it, is the reporter's duty to pass on to everyone whatever it is that he can find out about the men and ideas that affect their daily lives.

The assignment to Moscow was offered me in the summer of 1944. I accepted because I felt that any reporter who declined could never thereafter honestly claim to possess the curiosity which is indispensable to journalism. Some months intervened between the assignment and my actual arrival in Moscow in March, 1945. During that time I crammed on books about Russia. After my return in

April, 1947, I continued a year and a half on *Time*, engaged in a kind of post-mortem recapitulation and analysis of my censor-ridden Russian experience. Thus, I remained almost totally immersed in the subject for four years.

During that time the shape and content of the book I expected to write remained undecided. Then I undertook to deliver a series of ten lectures at The Johns Hopkins University. Once a week an audience containing teachers, professors, engineers, businessmen, United States Army officers, housewives, students, and even one farmer, one physician and a social worker, threw at me all the questions they could think of about the Soviet Union.

It was under their questioning that this book took shape. To me it seemed only logical to assume that the questions propounded by a group as socially and occupationally diverse as this one was, would also be the questions most other people wanted answered. Hence, the book to be done was one which provided the answers, and this, a compound of history, observation, and firsthand experience, is it.

CRAIG THOMPSON

Erwinna, Pennsylvania
September, 1949

The Police State

Chapter I

To PUT IT FLATLY, the people of the United States have failed to grasp the nature and meaning of the Communist party, a simple fact of complex causes and enormous consequences. The causes include good will, or a general unwillingness to face bad news; indifference, or a lack of effort to learn; optimism, or a desire to believe that all things work out well in the end, and naïveté, or the assumption that all other people are governed by the same moral values we prize and fight for. Being ourselves children of revolution who are still in search of a more perfect way of life, we are naturally benign toward other revolutionists who say they want the same things, and thus a perfect soil for mendacious propaganda which hides an ugly reality and promotes a fictional utopia. Moreover, this attitude is not restricted to the gullible alone; on an official level it has flawed the approach of the United States to the Soviet Union on many occasions in the past, and it will doubtless do so again in the future. The ultimate possible consequences can be total loss of the values we live by.

The Soviet Union's Communist party is called the All Union Communist party of Bolsheviks. Although the word Bolshevik is derived from the Russian word for majority, the Bolshevik party has never been a popular majority. Prior to the events of 1917 it was one of many splinter groups within the Russian revolutionary movement — the largest of them being the Social Revolutionary party with the Mensheviks next in size — and since its seizure of power in November of that year it has remained a very small splinter of the Soviet Union's population. Communism today does not reflect, and never has reflected, the political aspirations of a majority of Russians.

In its earliest rising Russia's revolutionary stream drew inspiration from the American and French revolutions. It first erupted in December of 1825 — causing among other things the formation of Russia's modern-style political secret police force by frightened Czar Nicholas I in 1826. For many decades after that it remained a semi-clandestine nether world of bubbling ideas and seething emotions.

Ideas fermenting beneath a blanket of police oppression can produce unpredictable events and strange men. The Russian revolutionary stream became cluttered with men who were basically individualists trying to recruit followers each to his own banner. There were democrats, anarchists, philosophical anarchists, terrorists, and in time, but especially after the publication of Karl Marx's *Communist Manifesto* in 1848, evolutionary socialists, revolutionary socialists, and only the All-Seeing Eye knows what else. Even the Dukhobors, an eccentric religious sect which voices social protests by mass undressing in public, came for a time under the suspicion of being a revolutionary organism, and, in an odd way, it was.

One product of the revolutionary stream was Lenin. Contrary to popular belief and Bolshevik dogma, Lenin was not pure Marxism in action. He borrowed much from Marx, it is true, but he also borrowed from Mikhail Bakunin and

Pyotr Tkachov, and from a nihilist named Sergei Nechiayev. Both Tkachov and Nechiayev are virtually unknown to readers of the English language. Very little of what they wrote has been translated, and there seems to be no biography of Tkachov in English. But Lenin many times told his secretary, Vladimir Bonch-Bruyevich, that Tkachov was unquestionably closer to "our," meaning his own, point of view than was Marx, and in his last years unflaggingly urged a study of Tkachov upon his associates. As a result today's Communism, which stems from Lenin, cannot always be understood by the light of Marx.

Although Lenin was an unpretentious man, he was a natural autocrat. Most of his life was spent in exile, either in Siberia or in the more salubrious atmosphere of Europe's capitals. He was a voracious reader and tireless scribbler and, like Marx, a man who could not abide dissent from any quarter. For one whose main enemy was the monarcho-capitalist world of his day, he fought with more sub-enemies than perhaps any other man of his age.

Revolution, to be permanent, needs a basic philosophy which can fire men's imaginations, and ultimately provide some satisfaction for their desires, but Lenin was only a pseudo-philosopher. His forte and his interest were tactics. Squatting in the bookstacks of liberal cities which gave him sanctuary, such as London, Paris, Zurich or Basle, he fought furious battles with an ink bottle for arsenal and a pen for artillery. In the whole directory of contemporary socialists there was hardly a one who was not, at one point or another, raked by his inky ire. But while he fought with his whilom friends and erstwhile companions, he dreamed of power.

It has been said, and with rare accuracy, that Lenin came out from behind the bookstacks and kidnaped a state. By early 1917 monarchical Russia was in a sorry plight. Three years of war with Germany in the Allied cause had created enormous manpower losses, with their attendant bereavement of towns and villages. Czarist Russia was not so backward, either industrially or socially, as Bolshevik propaganda now makes it out to have been. But it was corrupt at the top, bewildered in the middle, and seething at the bottom. Death and corruption had created a revolutionary situation and the revolutionary stream which had been swelling underground for nearly a century — with only a slight eruption in 1905 — burst to the surface and inundated the existing government. This was the first of two major events which occurred in Russia in 1917 and it amazed Lenin, then in exile, as much as it discomfited Czar Nicholas II, who was dethroned by it.

Almost as if in conspiracy, Bolshevik propaganda from Moscow and intellectual laziness here have caused most of us to forget that the first and the real Russian revolution occurred, not in November, but in February, 1917. That first revolution resulted in a genuinely democratic government, subject to all the stresses and infirmities of young democracy but pledged to a number of basic reforms. It abolished the secret political police, freed political prisoners, opened the press to all shades of opinion, and decreed genuinely democratic elections. But just as the revolutionary stream had contained a number of mutually antagonistic groups with the common aim of reform, so the new government was chivvied, tugged and weakened by a battle royal among power-seeking groups. By its own admission contained in an official party history* which, though now proscribed, has never been totally destroyed, Lenin's party at this time was among the smallest of the groups, with a mere 40,000 members. But it had Lenin.

In a sealed train, the Germans returned Lenin from Switzerland to Petrograd.† By sending him home, Wilhelm II's Imperial Command hoped to take Russia out of the European war then raging and so release German strength for an all-out drive against the West which had only recently received an infusion of new power due to the entry of the United States into the war. This hope was realized. One of Lenin's strong appeals to the Russian mass was his promise to take a war-weary people out of war.

Sometimes, in a revolutionary situation, slogans are as valuable as rifles. Masses can be manipulated with promises. Lenin made many promises, of which the two most important were "all land to the peasants," and "all power to the Soviets." In the Russian language, the word Soviet means council, and this was a promise that all government would be invested in the hands of local, regional, and national councils composed of deputies chosen by workers, peasants and soldiers. To the bewildered but angry Russian mass it

---

* "History of the All Union Communist Party," by A. Bubnov, in the *Great Soviet Encyclopedia.*

† In the tides of Russia's history Petrograd has had three names. It was built by Peter the Great and in his name called, with some canonical violence, St. Petersburg. When the revolutionaries who preceded the Bolsheviks came to power they called it Petrograd or, The City of Peter. After Lenin's death, it became Leningrad. Not long ago a whispered story that was popular in Moscow concerned a World War II veteran who was being interrogated prior to demobilization. The interrogation ran: Q. Where were you born? A. St. Petersburg. Q. Where were you educated? A. Petrograd. Q. Where were you mobilized? A. Leningrad. Q. Where do you wish to be returned? A. St. Petersburg.

had a powerful appeal, no less strong than the other chief slogan which promised land for nothing to the landless. The following Lenin's slogans attracted to Lenin's banner was big enough for his purpose — the seizure of power — but Lenin knew when he made them that the slogans were unrealistic and he must also have known that once they had served their purpose and he was in the saddle, they would have to be cynically repudiated, as they in fact subsequently were.

Since 1944, governments and peoples have repeatedly shown surprise at the reiterated discovery that wherever they are, or may go, Communists will not be satisfied with anything short of absolute power. But the only thing surprising about this is the surprise itself. Any other Communist attitude would be a betrayal of what Lenin taught, a deviation from principles which would expose the deviator to disciplinary action. In countries where Communists do have power, discipline is often a matter of death.

On the morning of November 7, 1917, the day of the Bolshevik coup in Petrograd, Lenin showed up at the headquarters from which Leon Trotsky was directing the uprising. Trotsky had given the Petrograd newspapers a statement which strongly suggested that the Bolshevik plans would end in peaceful negotiation. In brittle anger Lenin demanded: "Are you agreeing to a compromise?" Trotsky's reply was no. He had, he said, given out the reassuring news in order to create a lull, thereby putting the Bolsheviks in an even better position for the general attack which was, at that moment, actually beginning. "Ah," Lenin replied, "that is good! That is very good — very good." To which Trotsky rejoined: "To fool the enemy — to get him to make a fool of himself — is there anything better than that?"

In this thirty-year-old scene we have an important key to a major Communist tactic as well as a Western weakness that has been repeated time and time again. The weakness is the belief that agreement with Communists can be gained by negotiation and preserved by treaty. No amount of demonstration to the contrary yet seems to have destroyed this dangerous fallacy; there are still people in all countries who think it is possible to "work with the Communists." The underlying reason for this error is that the whole of Western politics is rooted in the principle of compromise — the idea that by giving a little here and taking a little there a system of government can be achieved which will be both stable and equable through having the support of a majority of the people. The disciples of Lenin do not believe in this. They assert that their system and only their system is correct. To them compromise is only a stratagem, a device to fool the enemy and gain a more advantageous position for further attack.

In one respect the West is fortunate. By the study of history and analysis of Bolshevik behavior it can learn to understand and evaluate these moves in any given situation. For, since the Bolshevik coup in Petrograd in 1917, the Bolsheviks have shown virtually no flexibility or improvisation. Move follows move with mechanical automatism, each leading to the next move. To any person who knows their history, every punch is telegraphed, every shift in tactics is apparent even before it takes place. For thirty years the pattern has been frozen; the tactics of 1917 go on being endlessly repeated. Western civilization can be made safe if its peoples will make themselves familiar with the pattern.

One indispensible source is Lenin's book on tactics called *What Is to be Done?* Written in 1902, it is a diagram of Communism in which the nature and mechanism of the movement takes clear shape. Lenin denounced "freedom of expression" because, he argued, it really meant freedom to disagree and hence endangered discipline. He defined the function of the newspaper as the spinal cord of a revolutionary party. He demanded that this party be divided into two levels consisting of a visible, or legal apparatus engaged in seemingly innocuous political agitation, and a secret core of a dozen or so trained revolutionaries into whose hands all threads of activity would be placed, a full-time general staff as it were. He declared one of the functions of this mechanism to be the infiltration of all kinds of bodies such as trade unions, student groups and so forth. He denounced every argument which tended to establish the trade union as an economic group seeking economic betterment for workers as "capitulation and compromise" with capitalism. He said: "Attention must be devoted principally to the task of raising the workers to the level of revolutionaries and not to degrading ourselves to the level of the laboring masses." And, finally, he touched a talisman by pointing out that "the most diverse strata of society, year after year, advance from among their ranks an increasing number of discontented people who desire to protest." It made no difference whether the causes of discontent were economic, social, political or psychopathic — the big fact was that these discontented people could be trained to serve the eventual aim of revolution.

From 1900, when Lenin's doctrine began to take shape, until 1917, when the long-growing revolutionary situation in Russia finally ripened, Russians found Lenin's party among the least attractive of the several revolutionary parties in existence. The harsh uncompromising nature of Lenin's preachment repelled Russians then, even as it does reasonable men and women elsewhere today. Both the Menshevik and the Social Revolutionary parties showed far more gains than did the Bolsheviks. But the Bolsheviks agitated and propagandized more vigorously. They sacrificed honesty to noise, principles to expediency, truth to slander, and kept themselves alive by the systematic exploitation of the more violent and unscrupulous among the discontented. Although seldom dismayed by the failure of his program to enlist a mass following, Lenin did feel it necessary to examine this fact from time to time. To quote an official history:* "He explained it by pointing out that millions of people, inexperienced in politics, had awakened and pressed forward to political activity. They were for the most part small owners, peasants, workers who had recently been peasants, people who stood midway between the bourgeoisie and the proletariat. Russia was at that time the most petty bourgeois of all the big European countries. And in this country 'a gigantic petty bourgeois wave has swept over everything and overwhelmed the class conscious proletariat not only by force of numbers but ideologically; that is, it has infected and imbued very wide circles of workers with the petty bourgeois political outlook.' " Among these "millions" the Bolshevik party's mere 40,000

* *The Short History of the Communist Party of Bolsheviks.* By Joseph Stalin & others. Moscow, 1938.

members furnished statistical proof that it had been rejected by a people who, though largely in a revolutionary mood, wanted the revolution to provide a genuinely democratic way of life.

Between the first 1917 revolution in February and Lenin's return to Petrograd in mid-April, the Bolsheviks supported, in a limited, lip-service way, the provisional government headed first by Prince George Lvov and later by Social Revolutionary Alexander Kerensky. The German Imperial Command did more than merely return Lenin to Russia; it backed him up with German gold, to the extraordinary sum of 50 million gold marks, roughly equivalent to 10 million dollars. It is at this point that the oft-repeated pattern begins. Lenin began with the financial support of a foreign power. Every Communist coup in Europe since 1944 has had the support of Moscow in one or both of two kinds, money and/or the Red Army. Even in France, and probably elsewhere, the disruptive Communist programs have been given substantial financial help by Moscow.

From the moment of Lenin's arrival he declared war on the provisional government, and in a speech to his party lieutenants gave them a terrific tongue-lashing for even the lukewarm and tentative support they had been tendering the government. This talk, one listener said later, made it seem "as if all the elements of universal destruction had risen from their lairs, knowing neither barriers nor doubts, personal difficulties nor personal considerations."[*] It is a continuing reminder to us now that, although Lenin's return was widely noted in the Petrograd press, not a single foreign correspondent regarded the news as worth even a

[*] *Lenin, A Biography.* By David Shub. Doubleday & Co., New York, 1948.

line to his paper. They knew who Lenin was — they just didn't take him or his Bolsheviks very seriously; a mistake that has since been repeated many times.

With the help of the German money, the Bolsheviks rapidly expanded their propaganda machinery to a total of 41 publications. Russia was, in those short-lived days, a land of the completest freedom, and the Bolsheviks exploited that to the utmost. They did it on the basis of a program artfully contrived to build up chaos in an already chaotic situation. They attacked the provisional government as the tool of capitalism charging it with all kinds of dastardly plots against the people. They sent agitators everywhere — into the front lines among the soldiers half-heartedly fighting the Germans and into the reserve garrisons; the factories; among the peasants. These agitators were not concerned with telling a consistent story; their concern was solely to stir up indecision, discontent and hatred of the provisional government.

The Bolsheviks were active, determined, and they had a program. That program, of course, had only one objective, the seizure of power. But their even greater advantage was that they were not taken sufficiently seriously. Only Kerensky, darkly muttering that Lenin would destroy the revolution, seemed fully aware of the dangers. His colleagues in the government pooh-poohed his forebodings. The increasing effect of the Bolshevik propaganda did disturb them — but, such was their visionary and real love for the newly gained freedom they enjoyed, they could not bring themselves to deny any part of it to anyone. They were hamstrung by the shibboleths of democracy.

Toward the end of June — two months after Lenin's

return — the Bolsheviks moved toward their first real test of the provisional government. They summoned a "demonstration." Slogans and placards were prepared: "Down with the ten Capitalist Ministers!" "End the War!" "No separate peace with Wilhelm," "All Power to the Soviets," "Bread, Peace and Freedom." These slogans are worth examination, both as reflecting the conditions in Russia, and the techniques of Lenin. In the first place the use of the word capitalist had a more direct appeal to the lowest levels of ignorance and poverty than it had application to the true complexion of the government. It was an appeal to blind hate. "End the War" was of course addressed to disaffected soldiers — to a class which was composed either of actual or potential deserters most of whom were, however, still in uniform and still possessed arms. Their enlistment in the Bolshevik cause was of enormous importance. But the next slogan flatly contradicted it. Since Britain, France and the United States were at that time Germany's other principal enemies, and since they had no intention of ending the war, the only possible way Russia could end its war was through a separate peace with Wilhelm, a peace which most Russians knew could be achieved only on the terms dictated by Germany. This kind of peace was precisely what Lenin intended to make and did later sign;* his use of the slogan was a deliberately lying appeal to the Russian masses who opposed such a course. The slogan "All Power to the Soviets" did not make sense from a Bolshevik point of view. Not only the national Congress of Soviets, but nearly all

* Negotiated by Trotsky at Brest-Litovsk and signed March 3, 1918. In the weeks following Lenin's seizure membership in the Bolshevik party shot up to 400,000. After Brest-Litovsk it dropped sickeningly to 115,000.

the local soviets were in the hands of Mensheviks and Social Revolutionary majorities, but the top power was on a dual plane — divided between the Congress of Soviets and the provisional government. Hence the slogan served to increase distrust and dissatisfaction with the government.

The Bolshevik program enunciated by these slogans was self-contradictory, mendacious and nonsensical. If the Bolsheviks had been seeking power by the peaceful means of attracting voting majorities the inconsistencies would have been emphasized or nullified by the operations of time and reality. Instead, they were recruiting a mob for violent action. In that mob they planned to place a number of armed persons and with it they planned to arrest the provisional government and seize power. The June plot was discovered and denounced and the Bolsheviks, getting cold feet at the last moment, cancelled it. But the aftermath was invaluable to them. Charged squarely with responsibility, they pretended innocence and cried that they had been falsely accused. Then one of them, Leo Kamenev, formally demanded that he be arrested and charged. The provisional government shrank from this course, either from distaste for the limitation of political freedoms, or from lack of legal evidence, but more probably from both. Thus the Bolsheviks discovered that the government was unwilling to take energetic action and they promptly launched an even more vituperative propaganda campaign against it by charging that it was preparing for civil war and seeking a pretext for disarming the workers and peasants.

In this renewed propaganda is revealed a continuing Bolshevik trick which still characterizes the propaganda behavior of the Soviet Union. Lenin knew full well that he intended to launch a civil war, and for that reason wanted to keep arms in the hands of the workers and peasants. So he charged his adversaries with planning civil war. Everywhere in Europe, in the wake of World War II, the Communists tried to follow the same course. In addition we see the same mechanistic method in many Soviet charges against the United States. Moscow intends to subject every European country it can to political and economic enslavement; hence it charges the United States with this design. Moscow has liquidated fewer former Nazis than any other occupying power in Germany; hence it charges the other occupying nations with gentle and favorable treatment of Nazis. Moscow is carrying on the greatest warmongering campaign of any of the world's nations; hence the fulminations of Soviet Foreign Minister Andrei Vishinsky — a cynical ex-Menshevik — against United States warmongers. As we should all know by now, a warmonger is anyone who opposes the designs of the Soviet Union.

In Petrograd, in the summer of 1917, these befuddling and inflammatory methods began to run ahead of Bolshevik preparedness. Propaganda among the soldiers garrisoned around the city had intensified and inflamed their war weariness. But the provisional government was trying to carry on the war even with home conditions of revolutionary disorder and division. On July 1, at Kerensky's orders, the Russian front commanders launched an offensive which was successful at first, then rapidly lost its punch. In Petrograd the sailors of Kronstadt, a naval base near the city, and the soldiers of several regiments which the Bolsheviks had converted, as well as the armed workers of the Putilov factory in which Mikhail Kalinin, later to be a Politburo

member, had been an old worker, chose July 17 as the day
for uprising.

The Bolsheviks were divided about assuming charge of,
and responsibility for, this attempted putsch. For this
reason they tried halfheartedly to assume control of it, and
halfheartedly to leave themselves in a position in which
they could once again deny responsibility. The uprising
was staged. Those who took part in it were chopped down
by the machine guns of troops loyal to the provisional government and it failed for lack of leadership and coordination.

This time the provisional government did act. Having
learned of Lenin's supply of German gold, the government
ordered the arrest of Lenin and others on a charge of plot-
ting to destroy the state at German behest. Lenin, knowing
what he would have done, remarked: "This time they will
shoot us."

But news of the warrant reached him sooner than the
officers did and he went into hiding. The Bolshevik party,
having been designed long before for just such an operation, took the revolutionary portion of its apparatus
underground.

Now Kerensky made a mistake which proved, in the end,
to be fatal. Concerned about popular unrest, military lassi-
tude, desertions and other defections at the front, he placed
a strong man, General Lavr Kornilov, in charge of the Russian armies. Hardly had he taken command than Kornilov,
who has been described as a man with the heart of a lion
and the brains of a lamb, adopted a course of action which
had the apparent purpose of destroying both the Bolsheviks and the provisional government. Today, in France,
many persons are describing General Charles de Gaulle

with a phrase the Russians used in 1917 to designate the
forces Kornilov represented — the phrase is "the third
force." As soon as he realized the magnitude of his mistake,
Kerensky not only relieved Kornilov of his command, he
also slammed him into jail. But irreparable damage had
been done. Kornilov's behavior had aroused genuine and
widespread alarm for the future of the revolution, and the
Bolsheviks now really had the opening they had been seeking and which, by the nature of their organization and the
singleness of their purpose, they were in a position to exploit fully.

Into their propaganda they now injected the note of "I
told you so." Despite Kerensky's arrest of Kornilov, Bolshevik propaganda adroitly made it appear that the two
were, in reality, coconspirators. In the Petrograd Soviet
Trotsky secured passage of a Bolshevik resolution for the
first time. The danger posed by Kornilov's actions caused
many Bolshevik opponents to adopt, at least temporarily,
the line that Lenin's group was the lesser of two evils. The
Soviet in Petrograd, and in other cities such as Moscow,
set up special committees to mobilize the people against
Kornilov. In Petrograd the committee was known as the
Military Revolutionary Committee, with Trotsky as its
chairman. This was the instrument that made the Bolshevik coup possible.

Long after Kornilov was in jail, this Military Revolutionary Committee went on making preparations to crush a
Kornilov mutiny. It sanctioned the creation of armed units
in the factories — later to be known as Red Guards. Then
it sanctioned the introduction of political commissars into
the military units, Trotsky taking good care to see that

these were trusted Bolsheviks. Bolshevik couriers raced
from city to city, keeping Bolshevik units informed of what
was being prepared. Lenin, who did not yet dare to return
to Petrograd, bombarded the Bolshevik Central Committee with letters some of which were so frantic and full
of whip-lashing urgency that they did not make sense. But
most of them did. The Bolsheviks at last, in the Petrograd
Military Revolutionary Committee, had the means of preparing a coordinated armed insurrection.

Lenin wrote: "We must . . . without losing a single
moment organize a staff to direct the insurrectionary
forces; distribute these forces; move the loyal regiments to
the most important points; arrest the general staff and the
government; move against the cadets and the Savage Regiment [troops known to be loyal to the provisional govern-
ment] such detachments as will die rather than allow the
enemy to reach the heart of the city; we must mobilize the
armed workers, call upon them to fight to the last desper-
ate battle, occupy at once the telegraph offices and the
telephone exchanges, install our own staff of the insurrection in the central telephone exchange and connect it by
wire with the factories, regiments and centers of armed
fighting."

Because the Military Revolutionary Committee, as an
arm of the Petrograd Soviet, had powers which were recognized as legal, it could organize the Bolshevik forces behind
a screen of official action. This was done by close coordination with the secret portions of the party apparatus. By
early November the Bolsheviks could count on a number
of military units in addition to sizable forces of Red Guards
which had been mobilized in the factories. In mid-October

Lenin had returned to the city from his hiding place, wearing a black wig over his bald head, and a dirty bandage round his face. He was more than ever impatient, and, although some among the Bolshevik leadership, notably Kamenev and Gregory Zinoviev, were still uncertain of the success of an armed insurrection, they were overridden. As always, Lenin had his way. November 7 was fixed as the day to strike.

From this distance of time and available knowledge, it now appears that the only things the Bolsheviks really succeeded in keeping secret were the day they intended to strike, and the extent to which they had succeeded in capturing some military units.

While all these preparations were going on, there convened in Petrograd a Democratic Congress, which was also known as the Pre-Parliament, and which, representing all shades of political opinion, was intended to serve as a sort of forerunner of a future parliament.

On the morning of November 6, 1917, Kerensky went before this group and told them that he had in his possession incontrovertible proof that Lenin and his comrades had organized an insurrection against the provisional government. He affirmed that the provisional government would fight to the end, and warned them that it could not hope to win unless it had the immediate cooperation of all the parties represented in the Pre-Parliament. In retrospect the action of this body seems fantastic — but no more so than the attitudes of certain Frenchmen and Italians today, and no more so than Social Democratic and democratic forces in various European countries during the past few years. The behavior of the Mensheviks and Social Revolutionaries in 1917 was duplicated, almost as if by slavish rote, by democrats and socialists in various European countries — Hungary, Rumania, Czechoslovakia — in 1946 and 1947, just as was the behavior of the Bolsheviks.

What this Pre-Parliament did was to debate all day, and then pass a resolution which, while it condemned the Bolsheviks, also condemned the provisional government. It affirmed: "If the Bolshevik movement is drowned in blood, then, whether the victory is won by the provisional government or the Bolsheviks the real triumph will belong to a third force which will sweep away both the Bolsheviks, the provisional government, and the entire democracy."

Faced with Kerensky's warning that the house was on fire, these gentlemen advised him to: (1) take immediate action to put large landed estates in Russia under the jurisdiction of local land committees pending distribution of the land to poor peasants; (2) take steps to hasten the convocation of a Constituent Assembly — the next necessary step toward permanent government — which then had not even been voted on by the Russian people; (3) ask all belligerent powers to begin peace negotiations immediately. These things, they said, would cause the Bolshevik movement to go into a decline and wither away.

Adding insult to flatulence a Menshevik named Theodore Dan personally delivered the Pre-Parliament's resolution to Kerensky and gave him a patronizing lecture. The Pre-Parliament, said Dan, was far better informed than was Kerensky, who, he asserted, was under the influence of reactionary interests and was exaggerating the dangers. Kerensky's attitude, he added, was making it difficult to "negotiate with the Bolsheviks concerning the liquidation of the insurrection."

In every Bolshevik coup since 1944 there is the repetition, in one form or another, of just such scenes. The benign men of good will who, from pooh-poohing the Bolshevik design, turn piously to the belief that negotiation is the cure for power lust, usually wind up in flight or before a firing squad.

At the very moment that Dan was delivering the lecture to Kerensky, Trotsky was sending out the following order to all military commands under the Military Revolutionary Committee:

"1. The troops which are guarding the approaches to Petrograd must be fully prepared for action.

"2. The guards at the railway station must be reinforced.

"3. Not a single military unit whose attitude toward present events is unclear must be allowed to enter Petrograd.

"4. Kornilov's [a code word for Kerensky's] troops must be detained by force if they do not submit to persuasion. Act sternly, but cautiously; resort to force where necessary.

"5. Immediately report all troop movements to the Military Revolutionary Committee in the Smolny Institute in Petrograd, and also send there representatives of the local soviets and regimental committees for purposes of liaison."

Next morning the Bolsheviks struck in force, and late that night they were in power. After an all-day siege, the Winter Palace, where the provisional government sat in helpless terror, fell, and the provisional cabinet was marched across the Neva River to imprisonment in Peter and Paul Fortress. Kerensky, alone, was not among them. Early in the morning he had driven through the Red Guard lines to military headquarters outside the city hoping to arrange for additional troops with which to quell the Bolshevik insurrection. He failed — not because the troops he sought were pro-Bolshevik, but because they cried a pox on both houses. By their refusal to take sides they handed the victory to Lenin.

The civil war into which Lenin that day plunged Russia lasted three years and spilled more Russian blood than had been let in the three-year war with Germany. By the time it ended Lenin had both an army and a formidable police force, and the Bolshevik grasp was too strong to be shaken off.

As this sequence of events shows, the Bolsheviks, but particularly Lenin and Trotsky, felt their way through this coup. But ever since, at the Lenin Institute in Moscow, Communists from all over the world have studied and restudied it and learned its lessons thoroughly.

Of course, some of the details change according to local conditions. In Czechoslovakia, for example, the Communists did not have a Military Revolutionary Committee, nor did they have Red Guards. But the Communists did control the Ministry of Interior, and through it they built up a corps of trusted people who could be armed, while for the party apparatus the so-called action committees performed the same recruiting and policing function for the Czechoslovak Communists that the agitators in regiments and factories had performed for the Russian Bolsheviks. And when the non-Communists among the Czechoslovak government were confronted with the iron choice of submission or blood, they backed away from bloodshed. Communist boss Klement Gottwald and company in Czechoslovakia no more represented a majority of Czechs than had Lenin and company represented a majority of Russians.

The principal elements of the pattern are easily isolated and constant. They are:

1. The structure of the Communist party.

2. The determination of the Communists to gain total power regardless of what it may cost in bloodshed or damage to a nation's welfare.

3. The mendacious and wholly irresponsible use of propaganda to generate division among the people, engender hatred between classes or groups, and induce indecision among the more responsible.

4. The advantage Communism gets from the fact that its topmost leaders are invariably intensively trained full-time professional revolutionaries.

5. The inability of non-Communists to believe that Communists are really that way. Communists are seldom opposed by their own weapons or methods simply because these weapons and methods are repugnant to the people who oppose Communism. Hence Communists have the advantage of knowing that the adversary will always be soft, vacillating and undecided. Therein lies at least half their strength.

Chapter II

IN CONSIDERATION of the recurrent waves of bloody terror which constitute the dominant fact of the thirty years' history of the Soviet Union, it is necessary always to remember that false promises make for violence, violence generates hate and repression, and that rule by terror, once begun, can be sustained only by more terror. It is often argued that what has happened in Russia since 1924, when Lenin died, is due to Josef Stalin's iron fist. Lenin, this argument runs, was a good and worthy man, only Stalin is evil; Lenin's "revolution" was good and Stalin corrupted it. The argument is misleading. Everything that has happened since Lenin, was inherent in Lenin's tactics.

The main fact was that by the use of violence and false promises, Lenin pinched off the head of the only democratic state in Russia's history and put himself and his small group in its place. He knew that his hold upon the state was weak and nervous, and to maintain his grasp he had to set about the ruthless liquidation of all those who might try to shake him loose. Precisely because his group was small, his methods had to be decisive. To quell his opponents, who included monarchists, capitalists and socialists of many shades, he reinstituted the secret police, even using a few of the Czar's hated personnel to do it. He also reinstituted state censorship in order to deny to others the press freedom which had been so valuable to his own design. In eight months Russia passed from czarism, through an interlude of the freest kind of individual liberty into a Leninist-Communist repression which was far more bloody, brutal and absolute than any the Czars had ever imposed.

It is history's jest that one of the more colorful accounts of this transition was written by one David Zaslavsky. In his later years, as a Moscow journalist, an editor of the Communist organ *Pravda* (Truth), and a man of no discernible scruples whatever, Zaslavsky was among the loudest, most vituperative and poisonous of the tub thumpers for Communism the world knew. But he was not always a Communist, nor did he always worship Lenin as he later pretended to do. In 1917, Zaslavsky was an executive of the Jewish Bund, which was one of the Marxist revolutionary splinter parties, and an editor of its party organ. He was then one of Lenin's most outspoken opponents.

Thirteen days after Lenin's coup, Zaslavsky screamed aloud in his little newspaper: "Lenin has taken power to become the genuine autocrat of Russia. . . . So far only the bourgeois press has been extinguished. . . . But which of the Czarist satraps has not swaggered over the press?"

This startled cry of pain was followed five days later by another: "Lenin and Trotsky are only the forerunners of frightful terror."

Again, a little later: "In Petrograd the Bolsheviks are closing up the press with sadistic cruelty indeed."

Still later: "Lenin's acts have become so thickly smeared with dirt that even Schneur [a notorious Czarist police agent] now feels as if he is among his own people."

And last: "Preliminary censorship! All fools and scoun-

drels have protected themselves by this instrument. Let
Metternich's shadow shade Lenin's head." And to all this
the shrewder and tougher Lenin answered: "Political
blackmailer. Capitalism purchases the Zaslavskys in its
own interests."

These words were spilled within six weeks of Lenin's
coup. They show not only what Lenin's methods were, but
also that in thirty years the words used in exchanges of
invective between Communists and anti-Communists have
changed little. The same words Lenin used against Zaslavsky in 1917, were used by Zaslavsky against Wendell
Willkie and many another American after 1944. But Lenin
had more weapons than words. His censors hounded Zaslavsky and his little paper from cellar to cellar. As one
means of evading suppression, the name of Zaslavsky's
paper was changed from *Dyen* (Day) to *Noch* (Night) to
Pol Noch, which means midnight. Soon thereafter darkness engulfed it altogether. It was then that Zaslavsky, to
use an official phrase, "re-examined his political beliefs"
and threw himself on Lenin's mercy. Zaslavsky applied for
membership in the Communist party, and Lenin, who had
need of many pens like Zaslavsky's, sanctioned a condi-
tional reprieve. From then on Zaslavsky's personal safety
depended on how well he served his Communist masters,
and this was the man who, year in and out, told his Soviet
readers that American journalists who said mean things
about Lenin or the Soviet Union were prostitutes.

The reason which impelled Zaslavsky to submit to con-
version is reflected in a sharp and horrifying vignette of
Lenin at this period which has come down to us from
Louise Bryant, widow of the John Reed who wrote *Ten*

Days that Shook the World, and later the wife of former United States Ambassador to Moscow William C. Bullitt. She describes * a scene in which Felix Dzerzhinsky, the frail, ascetic, fanatical boss of Lenin's secret police, brings to Lenin a list of the latest arrests and Lenin, scanning it, calmly orders: "It would be better to shoot two, hold these five, and let the rest go."

During the six years and three months that Lenin remained Russia's autocrat, his energy was divided between maintaining his power and trying to create the "socialist" state. When he turned from the dispensation of terror his precept for constructive action was one he borrowed from Bakunin: "To hell with the people. The public does not know what is good or bad for it."

This attitude has given a bad time to Lenin's apologists, and particularly those of the fellow-traveling fringe who talk about, and occasionally seemingly believe in, honest democracy. They call it a necessity, and claim that it was made necessary by Russia's backwardness. But for Russia and Russians, the sad truth is that though Lenin knew a great deal about the uses of terror, he had only the haziest ideas about how to create a socialist or any other kind of state. Perforce, he had to play his composition by ear, and the result became an awesome medley of trial and terror.

The Kronstadt uprising of March, 1921, is nowadays mostly forgotten, or deliberately overlooked. In this, the same Kronstadt sailors who had been so instrumentally valuable in giving Lenin power in 1917 revolted against him and tried, by force of arms, to put an end to his regime.

---

* *Mirrors of Moscow.* By Louise Bryant. Thomas Seltzer & Co., New York, 1923.

Behind the uprising was the land policy. The men of Kronstadt were largely from the villages, and from their homes they had been receiving horrendous tales of starvation. Their peasant fathers and brothers had received, or taken, the land. But, in turn, the state was taking by requisition nearly everything they produced on the land, and this was a revolutionary result for which they had not bargained.

Led by Trotsky and Zinoviev, the newly created Red Army quashed the ex-heroes of Kronstadt in blood, and Lenin, taking heed of the lessons it taught, inaugurated the New Economic Policy, or NEP, which had the basic effect of permitting the people, and particularly the peasants, a limited degree of free enterprise.

One disturbed witness * of the Kronstadt mutiny wrote in his diary: "Who has won here, and who has been defeated?" Lenin's new state was still very young then, and the answer was not, perhaps, so obvious. But now it is. At Kronstadt, a dictatorship won and the people were defeated. It was only another manifestation of what began in 1917 and has been continued, in big and little ways, ever since.

In retrospect Kronstadt also becomes an excellent sample of another Communist phenomenon—the creation of a demonology. The official version of Kronstadt is this: "A glaring instance of the new tactics of the class enemy was the counter-revolutionary mutiny in Kronstadt. . . . Whiteguards, in complicity with Socialist-Revolutionaries, Mensheviks and representatives of foreign states, assumed

---

* *Pattern for World Revolution.* By J. Rindl and J. Gumperz. Ziff-Davis. New York, 1947.

the lead of the mutiny. The mutineers at first used a Soviet signboard to camouflage their purpose of restoring the power and property of the capitalists and landlords. They raised the cry: 'Soviets without Communists.' The counter-revolutionaries tried to exploit the discontent of the petty bourgeois masses in order to overthrow the power of the Soviets under a pseudo-Soviet slogan."*

The meaning of this falsified history is that since the Soviet dictatorship presents itself to its people as the most perfect state, it cannot admit its imperfections. Failures and disasters cannot be truthfully confessed as the result of mistakes, but must be presented as the work of enemies. From then until now, everything that goes wrong is blamed on foreign agents. When the police cannot honestly find a spy cozily nestling in some Moscow hostel, poisonously spreading a deadly web of popular discontent, they have to make spies out of whatever material they have at hand, as, within recent times, they did with the inoffensive National Broadcasting Company correspondent Robert Magidoff, and the bewildered, utterly loyal-to-Stalin Anna Louise Strong. Who knows when Stalin might need another peg on which to hang another bloody massacre of his own people?

In many respects Stalin is what he claims to be, the loyal disciple of Lenin and the continuer of Lenin's policies. But in many others he is an innovator and disciplinarian who has raised the ancient precept of rule by division and terror to the level of a modern, if hideous, art.

Stalin is a Georgian, born in the Transcaucasian hills which, since the beginning of history, have stood at the

* *Short History of the Communist Party.*

junction of human tides from East, Middle East, North
and West. His father was a drunken cobbler, his mother a
woman of Orthodox piety. His formal education was training for the clergy, and his lifelong pride was his Tartar
blood which, he felt, made him more an Asiatic than a
European. The historical grooves his mind fitted most
snugly where those channeled by the leaders of the Mongol
horde, men of ruthless ambition who carried the banners
of the barbaric East as far westward as the Danube, and as
far north as Moscow.

Stalin, one of the most rigorous disciplinarians in history,
claims to have left the seminary in which he was a student,
at the age of seventeen, because he could not abide the
discipline the monks enforced. This is probably one of his
statements that is true — it is in character.

The earliest records of his party activity show him to
have been an ambitious youth who advanced his own
designs by stealth, connivance, and double-dealing. The
party members of Tiflis, where he first became politically
active in a revolutionary way, read him out of their group
after a party trial in which he was convicted of having
falsely slandered the group's leadership with the aim of
deposing it. Later, he used the same method to get rid
of Trotsky, and still later to provide grounds for executing
some of those who sided with him against Trotsky.

Never an intellectual, Stalin paid little heed to the great
battles over theory in which Lenin delighted. He wrote
very little, and that little was dull and inconsequential.
Even within the party Stalin was, for many years, more
an underground figure than anything else. His specialty
was "expropriation," a high-sounding, self-justifying word

used to designate the highway robberies by which party
funds were often obtained. In these he was always the man
who laid the plans, engineered the coups, and got the
money, but never one to stand in the front lines and throw
a bomb.

Stalin's climb to power was predicated upon his political
acuity. While Lenin lived, Stalin was content to serve as
party secretary, a job most high-ranking Bolsheviks regarded as a thankless, paper-shuffling form of drudgery for
which obscurity was the principal reward. But Stalin
used it to distribute important jobs to people he thought
he could rely on, and when the test came, as it did after
Lenin's death, he had a well-placed, loyal political army
to help him win his fight with the brilliant, intellectually
superior Trotsky.

Stalin's reign, like Lenin's, has been bolstered by a
political police, an army, and a self-styled "elite" which
calls itself a political party and is, in fact, a semi-secret
society with military discipline. Within months after taking
power, Lenin signalized his break with everything that
was past by changing the name of this party from the
Russian Social Democratic Workers' Party of Bolsheviks,
to the Communist Party of Bolsheviks. Outside of Russia,
Communists long ago quit using the word Bolshevik and
tried to discourage its use by others. But in Russia, Communist and Bolshevik are commonly used, and inter-
changeable — two words for the same thing.

When Lenin died, the Communist party had already
become a world organization, governed from a central
headquarters in Moscow called the Communist International, or Comintern, to which the branches in various

countries sent their delegates. Central leadership then, as now, was predominantly Russian, but the local and national parties outside Russia enjoyed a large degree of autonomy and local freedom of action. The common aim then was world revolution as it is now, but each national grouping then retained the right and privilege of pursuing this aim in the manner it thought best suited to local circumstances. Stalin's most remarkable achievement is the fact that he took this loosely strung international organism and re-created it in his own image.

His method everywhere was the same one he employed in Tiflis in his youth and in Moscow in his maturity. By the use of baseless slander and conniving intrigue he first contrived to split the non-Russian national groupings, and then went on to eliminate, by whatever means, those who were not demonstrably and utterly pro-Stalin. If elimination required murder, and in Stalin's view it often did, then murder was committed—in Germany, Switzerland, Mexico, the United States, China and elsewhere. Sometimes, as in Germany, the ruthless pursuit of this course involved the wrecking of the national Communist party. To Stalin this was always a secondary consideration; what he wanted, and got, was unquestioning loyalty.

By degrees he transformed the organism that Lenin left into the largest, most fantastic and fanatic fifth column in history. The national non-Russian parties continued to behave like political parties where they could, as in France, Britain and the United States, and carried on agitation and political activity to the limits the laws of such countries allowed. But they also, in the classic pattern prescribed by Lenin, developed secret members whose duties were infiltration of governments, trade unions, trade associations, consumer unions, cooperatives, foundations engaged in social and political research, societies devoted to international exchange of ideas and information — into any and every place, in fact, where it was felt that Stalin's cause could be served. One purpose of infiltration was to place Stalin's agents in policy-making positions, in order to ensure that policies would favor Stalin. The other was to steal diplomatic, state, and technical secrets for Stalin's use.

All over the world this process succeeded to a degree beyond anything most people believe possible or credible. The greatest degree of success was achieved in those countries in which the individual enjoys the greatest degree of freedom — such as the United States. Free people prefer not to be suspicious, and are therefore the easiest to attack by stealth and surprise.

Naturally, this helps explain Stalin's spy complex, which to an American is one of the most absurd, bewildering and infuriating elements in the Moscow atmosphere. Knowing his own extraordinary success in planting or recruiting spies abroad, and having a propensity for limitless, evil intrigue, Stalin is just the man to find intrigue in stones and spies in everything.

Inside the Soviet Union, the Communist party has grown to 6,000,000 members, which roughly means one party man for each two political prisoners in Soviet slave-labor stockades.

Theoretically this party is a democratic institution, the members of which elect from among their numbers some 70-odd persons to serve on a Central Committee. In turn, and again in theory, the members of the Central Com-

mittee elect a small group to function as a Political
Bureau — called the Politburo. But in fact the party elects
nobody. Vacancies on the Central Committee are filled by
appointments by the Politburo. The Politburo also fills
vacancies in its own ranks. And in the Politburo, Stalin's
word is final. Thus the Communist party of the Soviet
Union, like all others, is nothing more than a carefully
selected and constantly purged instrument in Stalin's
hands. And it will remain that in the hands of whoever
succeeds Stalin for it is only by this monolithic, autocratic
control that power can be maintained for the man who
wields it. If the party operated on a basis of genuine
democracy, its leader might, from time to time, be
dethroned. No man who possesses the tenacity and ruthlessness to rise to the top of this heap would ever take
such a chance.

Stalin does not regard it as a party — he thinks of it as
an army. He has described it as consisting of a small group
of generals at the top, several hundred field-rank officers
under that, perhaps 20,000 lieutenants and captains beneath them supported by 100,000 to 150,000 noncoms. The
rest of the Soviet Union's 6,000,000 party members are
shock troops with another 10 million members of the
Young Communist League as reserves.

Martial law always suspends constitutional law when it
is imposed in countries where constitutions exist. Hence,
in Stalin's view, the Soviet Union is always in a state of
martial law, and the written constitution always in a state
of suspension for the martial party. For example, the USSR
constitution guarantees to everyone the right to worship.
The Communist party forbids its members to worship any

god, whether Jesus, Jehovah or Mohammed, for the stated
reason that Marx decreed religion to be the opium of the
masses but actually for the more realistic reason that the
Communist party cannot, in its terms of discipline, permit
any member to put any god before it.

In the Communist party discipline is god next to Stalin,
or more properly, they are the same thing. A Communist
may not question an order, but only obey. He may not
resign, for that would be desertion. When Stalin said, as
he did in 1939, that party membership is a life-and-death
matter, he meant a good deal more than most non-Communists read into his speech. He meant, in fact, that backsliders must be isolated or dispatched.

The process of becoming a member of this "elite" is akin
to attaining membership in a secret society. Mostly candidates for membership are elevated from the ranks of its
junior auxiliary, the Young Communist League, which is
made up of young people mostly between the ages of fourteen and twenty-five. Each new party member must have
a proposer and a seconder. Functionaries of the unit in
which he is proposed bear the responsibility of giving the
candidate a thorough investigation, particularly to determine his habits and attitudes of mind. Complete loyalty
to Stalin and an automatically reflexive ability to interpret
all problems and events in the argot of historical materialism are the most desirable qualities a candidate can
possess. Finally, before membership becomes official, a
candidate must remain on probation for a period of time
which has varied at various periods and is currently one
year. About the only things missing are the sheets and

hoods of the Ku Klux Klan, and the ritualistic blood mingling of the Mafia.

In return for the loyalty and discipline the party commands, party membership pays off in material advantages. When better jobs are to be filled, party members are most likely to get them.

Although Communists will be found in all branches of activity, from the arts and sciences to factory labor, the greatest concentration is in the bureaucracy. Basically, this party, above the written Soviet constitution and responsible only to the Politburo, runs the Soviet Union's organs of administrative government.

The Politburo is above the government and out of reach of the people. It cannot be questioned, challenged or criticized, and so the state, as such, has neither identity nor authority. It is simply a chattel of the Communist party — an enormous chattel containing 190,000,000 persons covering one-sixth of the earth's land area whose reserves of natural wealth have hardly been tapped, much less exhausted.

For us, this gigantic reservoir has significance not alone because of its massive geography but also because it is in the hands of a group which is openly and unequivocally dedicated to the eventual aim of controlling the world. For us, it is necessary to think of the Soviet Union not as a sovereign member of the community of nations, but as the captive arsenal of world revolution.

The determination of the handful of men who comprise the Politburo to impose upon the world the kind of government they now impose on the inert, patient mass of people in the Soviet Union has brought the peoples of the non-Communist world to a fateful place. They have two courses — they can accept Communism or combat it.

This is a choice about which too many people are still confused. When a citizen of the United States goes into the market place to buy, he usually insists upon a pretty thorough examination of the article he intends to purchase. Though it is possible to judge an automobile by the way it runs, or a hat by the way it fits, looks and feels, none of these criteria are a sure way to judge Communism. In this field, and for many years, objectivity has been virtually lost in the hot mists of propaganda, apology and revulsion.

These feelings have their roots in political prejudices of one kind or another. They are difficult to lay aside because they are difficult for the individual to recognize within himself. But if a person shops for a political system with the same attitude he or she uses when shopping for a hat, or home — that is, simply by asking himself, "Can I live with this? Is this the one for me?" — preconceptions and prejudices fade and the choice becomes easier. Where Communist party rule is concerned, as it is here, the only shopping place is the Soviet Union, because only there has it been in power long enough to prove beyond argument what it really is. We can find out what it will do here by seeing what it has done there. The time to find out is now — the fateful choice which the Communist party has thrust upon the world cannot any longer be delayed.

Chapter III

THE SIZE of the Politburo has varied at various periods, and at the present time (September, 1949) it is composed of nine men with three more serving as alternates. These twelve are the most powerful men in the Soviet Union, and by that token, men whose thinking, behavior and decisions have a direct influence on your life and mine. Yet, very few people in the United States, or anywhere else outside of the Soviet Union, even know all their names. The names are:

> Josef V. Stalin
> Viacheslav M. Molotov
> Klementy Y. Voroshilov
> Andrei A. Andreyev
> Lazar M. Kaganovich
> Anastas I. Mikoyan
> Nikita S. Khruschov
> Lavrenty P. Beria
> Georgi M. Malenkov

> THE ALTERNATES:

> Nikolai M. Shvernik
> Nikolai A. Bulganin
> Alexei N. Kosygin

Now that Stalin is seventy, and not always in the best of health, speculation around the world turns repeatedly to the question of his successor.

Until the death, in 1948, of Politburo member Andrei Zhdanov, his name was most often mentioned as the probable future dictator. Zhdanov was the man who advocated the Stalin-Hitler pact, and sparked the 1939-40 winter war against Finland. Men who love peace may rejoice that he is dead, but his death has not resolved the speculation.

In many of Zhdanov's meddlings with Russia's internal problems, observers thought they saw preparations for a future contest for Stalin's job. In the purges of literature, the arts, and sciences it appeared that Zhdanov was trying to find cause to replace appointees loyal to Molotov or Malenkov, with men who would be loyal to him. If this was true, and there is much proof that it was, Zhdanov's death leaves Molotov a comparatively clear field, a situation in no whit disturbed by his recent relinquishment of the Foreign Minister's post.

Molotov's succession will depend on how much longer Stalin lives and rules, for Molotov is only ten years younger than Stalin. If Stalin should die soon, it is most likely that Molotov will take his place, while beneath him the real fight for the job will develop among the younger and more vigorous of those in line. Above all other certainties in this picture, one is that whether Molotov serves for a time, or does not, Stalin's eventual replacement will come from among the Politburo's present twelve.

Considered in this light, certain of the Politburo members automatically can be ruled out. Voroshilov, Andreyev, Shvernik and Kosygin do not have the brains and cunning to win such a contest. Kaganovich and Mikoyan, though smart, are no more likely to win because of other reasons; Mikoyan because he is fifty-five and an Armenian; Kaganovich because he is fifty-seven and a Jew. Khruschov will doubtless remain the head man in the Ukraine — a big job in itself considering that the Ukraine is a nation of 40 million people and contains a sizable segment of population always opposed to Russian domination, and always in a passively resistant mood which could, at any time, flare into active opposition.

Thus there are left only Beria, Malenkov and Bulganin and of these Malenkov is the youngest (forty-five), the toughest, the most adroit and the most likely winner.

But all conjecturing must remain merely that. Too many things can happen to change the circumstances. For several years prior to the spring of 1949 the Politburo contained a tenth full member whose name was Nikolai Voznesensky, the Chairman of the State Planning Commission. Then, suddenly, as is Stalin's way, Voznesensky was deprived of his job and dropped without explanation. Since Stalin has seldom chopped off the heads of his top henchmen for mere inefficiency or administrative misfeasance, and has always ruthlessly done so at the merest hint of disloyalty, the secret of what happened to Voznesensky may well be tied to a behind-the-scenes jockeying for position among Stalin's potential successors. The supposition is pure conjecture, but Voznesensky's sudden, unexplained disappearance is typical of what can happen to the men who help Stalin run Russia.

The Politburo is precisely what its name suggests, a policy-making board. It is the place where the party's problems, both internal and external, domestic and foreign, are discussed and decisions taken. Its sessions are secret, its minutes are never published, and its decisions become known only as they mature into action by one or another state organism or are made known in the form of decrees issued by the Central Committee of the party or the Council of Ministers of the visible government. In the Soviet Union's peculiar version of "democracy" the Politburo is the place where all the threads of power, like a puppet's strings, are drawn together into one manipulating hand.

The Politburo meets at regular intervals, and otherwise on call, in a big room in one of the Kremlin buildings and around a big table. The members and alternates attend with bag carriers, prompters, special advisers and bulging satchels. They seat themselves clockwise in the order of the alphabet, but the clock runs backward from Stalin's place.

Stalin's dominance is quiet, rather than assertive. The other Politburo members provide him with a real and valuable service. By debating vigorously among themselves, advocating alternative courses of action, suggesting compromises, and backing up their arguments with whatever research they can marshal to support their contentions, they help him make up his own mind. All decisions are his, and all are final. Once Stalin has spoken, all differences are automatically dissolved. Whatever the decision may be, or however much an individual Politburo member may oppose it, once it is taken its fulfillment becomes a matter of party discipline.

From time to time one hears talk, sometimes in well-informed circles, of a split in the Politburo. Such talk has had the Politburo members deeply divided over the question of whether the Soviet Union should continue its concentration of resources on heavy industrial expansion which is necessary to war, or turn some of its energies and materials into a larger and more vigorous effort to raise the living standard of Soviet citizens.

Such a division of opinion could easily exist, and exist for years, without ever leading to anything more than loud words across a table.

The Soviet Union possesses no machinery by which one political leader can ask for a public endorsement of his policy. Nor is this regime likely to set up such machinery for it knows that this would be the quickest way of putting itself out of business. Any other kind of active dissent is equally unthinkable. No living member of the Politburo is ever likely to forget that between the time Stalin began reaching for absolute power in 1924 until the purge had run its course in 1939, no less than nine members of this highest of all Soviet ruling bodies died violently — seven of them before firing squads, one by assassination in exile, one by his own hand.

The nine who died had one thing in common, Stalin distrusted them. One of them was Alexei Rykov, who had been the Soviet Union's Prime Minister and more than once was helpful in Stalin's battle against Trotsky. When the time came for Stalin to push Rykov aside in order to make Molotov prime minister, Rykov was not backward in reminding him of those past services. Stalin replied: "That's water over the dam. No Tartar gives a copper for that."

No other country in the world possesses a group at once so powerful and so little known as the Politburo's twelve. Nor is it likely that there is anywhere else a group which, in addition to doing most of its work together, relies so completely on each other's company for playtime relaxation. It is hardly conceivable that any one of them could have a thought which he had not, voluntarily or involuntarily, shared with the rest.

Whatever they share, it is only among themselves. Their lives are fantastically aloof from the people they govern. The Kremlin, where much of their work is done and where most of them also have apartments, is a high walled compound containing a number of buildings. In other days, in the days of the feared, fearful and oppressive Czars, the Kremlin gates were always open and any citizen could walk through, stopping perhaps for a quiet prayer in the Cathedral of the Assumption where every Romanov since Boris Godunov had been crowned, or gawking at the world's biggest bell which never pealed a note, or at what was once the world's biggest cannon that never fired a shot.

Russia's history is one of bloody violence with many grand-scale aspirations and many grand-scale frustrations, and much of the blood was spilled upon or within the Kremlin walls. The Kremlin, with all its tragic reminders, is an historical shrine which rightly belongs to all Russians, but since the rise of the Bolsheviks only a comparative handful have been able to set foot in it. It is closed to the public, and its gates are perhaps the most heavily and competently guarded portals anywhere.

Even on such occasions as sessions of the Supreme Soviet, the so-called legislative body of the Soviet Union, entry is only by special passes handed out by the security police. At the gate, pass-holders show their tickets and their ordinary passports. Packages, brief cases or typewriters they may be carrying are minutely examined. Though they are not frisked, pass-holders are asked if they carry weapons. Once inside the visitor encounters a uniformed security cop every few feet, each with rifle and bayonet fixed in addition to sidearms. More, these guards are all officers or noncommissioned officers. None are privates. The Czars were never so securely protected, but it is also true that in more than 300 years of Romanov rule there were fewer assassinations of royalty than there have been of top-ranking Bolsheviks in the past thirty.

Each Politburo member has his *dacha*, or country house, and these, too, are largely grouped in one area outside Moscow, along both sides of the road to Mozhaisk. Most of these houses are grandiose. Molotov's, seen from a distance across a low, flat meadow, bulks large, white, semi-modernistic. Reportedly it contains 40 rooms — but it is certainly no grander than some others. Stalin's is concealed behind a high brick wall complete with gatehouse and sentry box.

The route to and from this *dacha* area is along a street called the Arbat. Late at night, usually any time between 11 P.M. and two or three A.M., police appear by the scores along the Arbat. Traffic approaching it from side streets is shunted off. Residents on the Arbat overlooking the thoroughfare are required to keep their windows closed. Traffic that enters the street from either end at this dead hour is not permitted to stop.

During these hours the Politburo goes home, roaring through the night and the near-deserted street in bulletproof American-made cars — usually Packards — with a guard-filled car ahead and another behind. Not far from the point where they leave the Arbat and enter the Moz-haisk road, a glass-smooth, asphalt highway branches gently leftward, and for some miles runs parallel to the main road. In a country notorious for execrable roads, this is a private raceway, reserved for the exclusive use of Stalin and company.

This sort of show has some interesting effects on ordinary Russians. Once, I casually asked my chauffeur if he knew the license number of Stalin's car. He replied with emphatic abruptness and vehemence that he did not. In a spirit of mischief I prodded him, suggesting that a man who had accumulated so many other odd, interesting, generally useless bits of knowledge, as he had, must surely have encountered that one. He became surly, then angry, and shouted with something not far from hysteria: "I don't know. I don't want to know. Period."

Several times a year, on May Day, Army Day, and the anniversary of the November 7th *coup d'état,* the Politburo, flanked by other party bigwigs of near-Politburo status, publicly presents its collective face. These are the occasions of the gigantic Red Square parades. Red Square is a large, cobble-paved rectangular open space outside the Kremlin wall. Close to the wall, roughly equidistant from each end of the square, is Lenin's Mausoleum and near the top of the mausoleum, overlooking the square, is a kind of balcony, or tribune as the Russians call it. Here the Politburo lines up to receive the salute of millions of paraders.

As a display of that Russian flair for dramatic showmanship these demonstrations are in a class by themselves. But they have two aspects which are extraordinary. In the first place the security measures taken to make sure that no unauthorized, ordinary citizen gets anywhere near Red Square are more complete than anything I ever saw elsewhere. Hours before the leaders mount the tribune, every street leading to Red Square is closed off by a double line of security police. Persons leaving the Red Square area are freely passed, persons going toward it must show a special security police pass issued for that one occasion only. As a result, out of Moscow's teeming seven millions only a favored few thousand ever see one of these shows as a Red Square spectator.

But at the same time, factories and offices are closed down and their thousands of employees are required to report with families at specified points even earlier than on customary workdays. They are issued banners, placards, and gigantic portraits of the leaders and then they are marched to Red Square. Converging at the mouth of the square, marching between shoulder-to-shoulder lines of security police, they pour through for hours in a motley, straggling, orderless column which is impressive only for its sheer volume of numbers. This is, of course, the only time these tens of thousands ever get to see their rulers in the flesh, and many of them raise the familiar chant: *Slava Velikomu Stalinu, Slava, Slava, Slava.* (Meaning: Glory to Great Stalin, Glory, Glory, Glory.) Though Stalin revels in the glory, his glorifiers are still kept far enough away to make a tossed bomb impossible, and a pistol shot uncertain. The chances of an assassin getting on Red Square with a rifle are nil. Where Stalin is concerned even adoration must keep a safe distance.

The men on the tribune are not by any means craven

cowards. Even after thirty years, there is not yet one of them so young that he did not risk his life in revolutionary work or in the civil war which followed the *coup d'état*. Nor is that the only trait they have in common. Scanning that row of figures along the tribune one realizes that, except for facial differences, they are remarkably similar. This impression is bolstered by a reading of what little is available of individual biography on each of them. In fact, by selection of the bits of personal history, behavior, and physical appearance common to all of them, it is possible to draw a composite picture of a Politburo member which is as true of any one of them as his own individual biography — on the basis of what is known — would be.

A Politburo member is a short, heavy-jowled, heavy-bottomed man. His corpulence is more than half intentional since, in a hungry land, fatness bears its own testimony to good living and is the most striking evidence of privilege or power. But it is also evidence of an undisciplined appetite — a man to whom food is an escape from many other disciplines which must constantly be practiced. A Politburo member's character is best summed up by the same braces of adjectives which sum up Stalin: He is half-educated but clever, ambitious but provident, determined but sly, courageous and cruel, patient and vindictive.

Politburo members average fifty-six years and their average age on joining the Bolshevik party was eighteen and a half. As of 1949 this means they had six and a half years of underground experience before 1917. Thus they know from experience the techniques of underground agitation, such as how to form innocent-seeming workers' associations, societies, and even choirs and under the innocuous cover of these bodies to carry on Bolshevik agitation and propaganda. They have, also, inside knowledge of prisons and exile camps. Had not the liberal interim government which dethroned the Czars also thrown open jails and exile camps and freed political prisoners, many of them and particularly Stalin would not have been available to help overthrow, in its turn, that liberal government. They have been men of many aliases, and two of their number have given false names both to history and their children. Stalin's real name is Djugashvili and Molotov's is Scriabin.

Fawned upon, but feared and hated, their creed has been best stated by Bertolt Brecht, a German Communist poet, and translated by Ruth Fischer.* It is:

> "Who fights for Communism must be able to fight and not to fight, to say the truth and not to say the truth, to render and to deny service, to keep a promise and to break a promise, to go into danger and to avoid danger, to be known and to be unknown. Who fights for Communism has of all the virtues only one; that he fights for Communism."

But among these men this ruthless fight is often tempered by self-interest. In 1944, while the war was still on, one of their number, a man named Scherbakov, who since has died, appeared before a specially called meeting of party activists in Moscow and made an exhortatory speech calling for increased war production. "Factories," he said, "fulfill their total plan but do not produce the right quan-

* Ruth Fischer, *Stalin and German Communism: A Study in the Origins of the State Party.* Harvard University Press, 1948.

tities of various types of goods. . . . The aim of the moment is to produce more for the front."

Now it happened that at that moment the soldiers at the front were screaming for more spools to facilitate the stringing of wire between artillery observation posts and the batteries they directed. And in Moscow, at the factory where these spools were being made, work on them had been temporarily stopped while the workmen were diverted to the manufacture of a large order of upholstered easy chairs for Scherbakov. It was, obviously, only a pinpoint diversion in the total war production, but equally obviously, in view of his speech, it was a very large indication of Scherbakov's character. Yet, any Politburo member would have behaved as he did. In fact, it is that kind of behavior which makes them all fat men.

These, then, are Stalin's trusted helpers. They run the party and the apparatus of visible government.

The party organism next highest in functional importance to the Politburo is the Central Committee. Every member of the Politburo is a Central Committee member, but the total membership of the Central Committee is usually 71. Of this number, some hold portfolios in the visible government, a few are top-ranking military and naval men, and most devote their full time to party work.

The Central Committee directly controls seven major party organisms. These are:

1. The Administration for Cadres, which supervises the admission of new members, the purge of ideologically delinquent ones, and the activity of the Young Communist League.
2. Administration for Agitation and Propaganda, commonly

called the Agitprop section. This section supervises the
agitator, who functions in factories and offices as a combination lowest-level ideological snooper, party teacher,
backslapper and proselytizer and the propagandist whose
principal function is to propagate speeches, ideas and
slogans calculated to make the party more palatable to
the mass. There are many stories about these operatives,
but one I particularly like appeared in the Army newspaper *Red Star*. It concerned a Comrade Maksimov, who
after making a half-hour speech to a group of soldiers was
flabbergasted to discover that not one of them could
answer any question based on anything he had said.
With complete seriousness *Red Star* continued: "The
reasons were not far to seek. In the first place the group
leader had filled his speech with a mass of figures which
it was impossible to remember and his hearers had not
taken notes. In the second place the speaker had not
taken into account the political education of his hearers.
They had all been taken into the Red Army from the
western areas of the Ukraine [a Soviet euphemism for
former Polish territory] and consequently it was necessary to start from the very beginning as far as their political education was concerned. In the third place, Comrade
Maksimov spoke in Russian, and his hearers could not
understand him."

But the Agitprop section covers many other activities.
It is responsible for the ideological purity of art, music,
literature, and the conduct of the daily papers and magazines. Glavlit — or Chief Board for Literature — which
censors all matter for internal consumption as well as
export items such as the dispatches of foreign correspondents in Moscow — is part of Agitprop's responsibility.

3. Organization Bureau. This is the bureau which now has
   absorbed the old Comintern. It not only oversees organizational matters such as the assignment of important

comrades within the Soviet Union, it supervises the functional apparatus of Communism everywhere. Every important Communist in the world, and particularly those who have gone underground, has an up-to-date dossier in the files of the Orgburo.

4. Agricultural Section. This section is responsible for the operation and production of Soviet collective farms.

5. Schools Section. Significantly, there is no Ministry for Education in the Soviet Union's government that deals with elementary and secondary education although there is one for Higher Education. The lower schools, like the collective farms, are peculiarly the province of the party. I have never seen the name of anyone mentioned as head of the Central Committee's Schools Section, but Mrs. Kasenkina, the woman who jumped from a third-story window of the Soviet Consulate in New York to avoid returning to Russia, says that, preparatory to being sent out to New York as a Soviet teacher, she was interviewed by the then head of the Agitprop Section. This suggests that the Agitprop chief is also educational chief, which makes sense. The responsibilities of the two sections are not as far apart as might be supposed.

6. Military Committee. Party activity in the Red Army has now been made a separate, but parallel, party function. Although the fiction of democracy in the civilian party is still maintained, in the Red Army it has been abolished. There party functionaries are frankly appointed from above.

7. Control Commission. This is a kind of ideological audit bureau which checks on the work of all the other party organisms.

Over all these divisions, as well as all other Central Committee activities, there is a Central Committee secretariat composed of Stalin, Malenkov, and Georgi M. Popov, the "mayor" of Moscow.

It is within these organisms that most of the members of the Central Committee who do not hold government portfolios are employed.

Now that we have seen the main outlines of the party apparatus, and the extent of its ramifications, it is instructive to examine the top structure of the visible government, for it is this government that the Soviet Union presents to the world as the real organ of Soviet power.

It is, perhaps, necessary to define what I mean by visible government. I mean the commissioner of police as distinguished from the political party or group which may have given him his job, or, more explicitly, the man who actually holds the public office as distinguished from the party which may control him. Government by political clubhouses is certainly not unknown in the United States. But it is something most of our people have always rejected, fought against and often succeeded in curbing or eliminating. In the Soviet Union, on the other hand, it is the undeviating rule.

The Soviet Union's claim to world superiority in many fields is debatable or laughable, but concerning the number of its ministers there is no dispute. There are more ministers of something or other in Moscow than in any other capital of the world. The number varies from time to time because some ministries are often in the process of being merged at the same time that others, like the amoeba, are dividing but the list seldom dwindles much below sixty. Obviously, a cabinet of sixty ministers would be more nearly a congress and, as such, a manifest absurdity to anyone who wanted to get any work done. So, to carry on the work of this populous cabinet-congress, there is a kind of executive committee of the Council of Ministers, consisting of Stalin as chairman and nine vicechairmen. They do the business of the cabinet. Now, in one column we will list the twelve members and alternates of the Politburo, in the other the Council of Ministers' executive body. This is what we get:

Politburo (IN ORDER OF SENIORITY)	Council of Ministers (IN ORDER OF IMPORTANCE)
Stalin	Stalin (chairman)
Molotov	Molotov
Voroshilov	Beria
Andreyev	Andreyev
Kaganovich	Mikoyan
Mikoyan	Kosygin
Khruschov	Voroshilov
Beria	Kaganovich
Malenkov	Malenkov
	Bulganin
ALTERNATES:	
Shvernik	
Bulganin	
Kosygin	

In the Politburo, but missing from the Council of Ministers' executive, are Khruschov and Shvernik. Khruschov is chairman of the Council of Ministers in the Ukrainian Republic. Shvernik is president of the Supreme Soviet.

But even more illuminating are the names of those in the Council of Ministers who hold no portfolio in the visible government. Beria is, in fact, the boss of the two entwined police departments, but each of these has its own minister and Beria has no official title. Andreyev likewise holds no visible portfolio. He is head of the party's Agricultural Section and also of its Control Commission. Kosygin likewise holds no ministerial portfolio, but he is second in command to Andreyev in agricultural matters. Voroshilov functions as Stalin's proconsul in Budapest, presumably to keep an eye on Hungary's boss Communist Matyas Rakoczi. Kaganovich, in 1946, was sent to Kiev as a trouble shooter because, what with an industrial slow-down being staged by disaffected Ukrainian workers, and other disturbances, the task of keeping the Ukraine in order was too much for Khruschov alone. Later, he was recalled to Moscow. Lastly, Malenkov, like the rest, holds no place in the visible government, but gives his full time to running the party's Organization Bureau, the Cominform, and serving as second in command to Stalin in the party secretariat.

Thus, out of the ten-man directorate of the Council of Ministers, none is visibly connected with the visible government, yet each is a Politburo member engaged in supervising a segment of the government ministries.

The nature of this setup is worth establishing and re-membering largely because, from time to time, the Soviet government seeks to disclaim responsibility for acts of the Communist party, both inside and outside of Russia. Similarly, there are times when the Communist party pretends that it does not act for the Soviet government.

To accept such disclaimers it is necessary to believe that Stalin, as chairman of the Council of Ministers' executive, is capable of issuing orders and following courses of action which Stalin, the chief of the Politburo, does not know about and might not approve if he did. And vice versa.

Chapter IV

IN THE SOVIET UNION, the governmental organ which theoretically corresponds to the United States Congress, Britain's Parliament or The French General Assembly is called the Supreme Soviet. This organism is of particular interest primarily because it is used to generate the illusion that Russia's dictatorship has a foundation of popular support exercised through the democratic use of the ballot. As will soon be shown, this is strictly illusory.

The Soviet Constitution of 1936 defines the Supreme Soviet as the "highest body of state power" in the Soviet Union. The Constitution also provides that other governmental bodies, such as the Council of Ministers, shall give an accounting of their stewardship to the Supreme Soviet. Like other constitutional provisions in the Soviet Union, this one gets an occasional lip-service token but no real adherence.

The Supreme Soviet consists of two houses, one called the Soviet of the Union, and the other the Soviet of Nationalities. Members of the Soviet of the Union are "elected" on the basis of one deputy for each 300,000 of population, and the Soviet of Nationalities on a geographical formula which is intended to provide a certain equality of representation among the nearly 200 different national groupings which make up the Soviet Union. In the 1946 elections, there were 656 seats in the Union Soviet to be filled, and 631 in the Nationality Soviet.

Laws are deemed to have been enacted when a majority of both houses have approved them, and under laws already enacted either house may initiate legislation. During the past ten years the Supreme Soviet, in full session, has initiated nothing more permanent than ringing cheers for Stalin. Nor is there, during that period, any record of a single dissenting vote. The Soviet Union's Supreme Soviet is the world's biggest rubber stamp.

The session of March, 1946, is a typical example of its behavior.

Though Moscow contains nearly as many people as New York, its capacity to care for transients is less than that of Columbus, Ohio, or Atlanta, Georgia, and the task of housing and feeding 1,000 guests puts a real strain on its hotel facilities. Days before the deputies actually began to arrive one could feel them coming. The hotel service staffs took on an expectant tension. They polished floors, laid long white linen strips over the tired carpets in the corridors, chased away the last wisps of cobwebby dust, while telephone operators and reception clerks became distracted. The deputies poured in — big blond Balts and Ukrainians, swarthy Georgians and Armenians and so on down the line to little slant-eyed Mongols in large fur hats. There was a kind of uniform, unofficial but popular, that distinguished many deputies. It was a blue serge cap and a long, black or brown leather coat. All over the Soviet Union, but especially in the hinterland, this garb is especially favored by the lesser party chieftains.

Eventually they gathered in the rectangular, block-long, yellow, white and brown Andrievsky Hall of what used to be the Czar's palace and is still called the Great

Palace inside the Kremlin walls, to open their meeting. The deputies sat at school benches facing a stage on which the seats of the mighty rose in choir-loft tiers on either side of a wide aisle leading down to a podium equipped with two microphones — one for Radio Moscow and the other for the hall's amplifying system. A few minutes after the session was called to order, Stalin made his appearance, from a door at the back of the stage. He walked slowly, with a catlike step, his shoulders hunched slightly forward, to one of the rear benches. The delegates, and spectators in the balcony over their heads, came to their feet and a roar of handclapping filled the high vaulted ceiling. Standing, Stalin clapped his hands, too, and kept on clapping until he got tired, whereupon he sat down and the uproar subsided.

The session began with a reading of the agenda. It was unanimously adopted. Then followed a bill, already prepared, calling for the reorganization of the Council of Ministers. It, too, was unanimously adopted. Long, set speeches by various officials were interspersed between bits of business. As is the Soviet custom, speeches began and ended with perorations which, though they had a monotonous similarity, always evoked tumultuous and prolonged bursts of applause. A sample: "Our country has been able to proceed to a new five-year plan as a result of the victory won by the Soviet people over Hitlerite Germany and Imperialist Japan. We were victorious because our struggle on the front and in the rear was guided by a Man of Genius, the great strategist and leader of the peoples of the Soviet Union — Stalin." And so on to other items, other speeches, other unanimous votes until, in two or three days, the Supreme Soviet ran through a whole year of business and voted to adjourn, again unanimously.

In the periods between full sessions the business of the Supreme Soviet is carried on by a permanent presidium, the president of which is Politburo alternate Shvernik. Of all the Politburo members, Shvernik is the least important. At sixty, he has been on the list of Politburo alternates for nearly ten years, and been thrice passed over in the promotion to full membership of younger men with years less seniority. He is a bumbling, ineffectual, stupid man whose most pronounced trait of character is his undeviating loyalty to Stalin — the perfect bureaucrat and just the man to put in charge of a rubber stamp. But his job entitles him to be called the President of the Soviet Union.

The character of the Supreme Soviet is sufficiently suggested by the unanimity of its behavior, and its relative unimportance by the presence of Shvernik at its head. But it is necessary to analyze a Soviet election to see how it gets that way. For every top man in the Soviet Union — Stalin, Molotov, Beria, Malenkov, *et al.* — must be a deputy in one of its two houses else the fiction of representative government would become insupportably palpable.

The last general election in the Soviet Union was held on February 10, 1946. Watching it was like watching a miracle unfold, a miracle of organization, agitation and unanimity. Indeed, only once before in history had anything like it taken place, and that was in 1937 when the Soviet Union had its first election under the 1936, or Stalin, constitution.

The election was ordered by a decree of the Supreme

Soviet's presidium on October 5, 1945, which thus allowed a lapse of 128 days between the date of the decree and the day of voting; time in which to set up the machinery, make nominations, hold election meetings and all the rest. The purpose of the election was to fill the 1,287 places in the Supreme Soviet.

In the Soviet Union the first step in preparing for an election is the establishment of a central election commission which serves as an arbiter in all election matters for the whole country. This commission consists of fifteen members, and it is chosen by the Supreme Soviet's presidium from among lists of suggested names provided by many organizations. Principally, however, such lists are furnished by the Communist party, the Young Communist League, the party-dominated Central Council of Trades Unions, the party-manipulated unions of intellectuals such as the Writer's Union, the Artists Union, the Academy of Science, and by other party-controlled bodies such as Osoviakhim which, in the Soviet Union, is a permanent organization roughly analogous to our wartime Office of Civilian Defense. The result is that, from the very beginning, the election machinery passes into the absolute control of the Soviet Union's only political party. In this instance it was dominated by such upper-bracket party stalwarts as Popov, of the Central Committee secretariat, and Vasily V. Kuznetsov, a member of the party Organization Bureau, head of the Trades Unions Council, and guiding spirit of the Communist-run World Federation of Trades Unions.

That, however, is only the beginning. By a similar procedure, election commissions are established in each of

656 election areas from which the members of the Union
Soviet will be elected. The composition of these area commissions is naturally approved by the central commission,
and they in turn play a decisive role in the selection of the
precinct election commissions whose job it is to compile
the voting lists, serve as polling-place officials, and count
the ballots. It is on this precinct level that masses of people
are first offered the feeling of participation in a great
national event.

For example, the Dzerzhinsky area of Moscow had
places for 907 persons on its precinct commissions. When
the call for names went out, the party apparatus in the
district busied itself. It called a total of 474 meetings
which were attended by 21,000 persons, every seventh one
of whom made a speech. In the aggregate such figures
sound impressive, but a breakdown shows them to be
something else again. Since the election area contained,
roughly, 300,000 persons, only one in thirteen bothered to
attend the meetings, and this takes no account of those
who might have gone from one meeting to another. The
average attendance at each meeting was 46 persons, or
small enough to be easily manipulated by an experienced
party activist. Since no meeting need decide on more than
two names, these could easily have been agreed upon in
advance, and people to propose the names placed in the
audience. At this stage two things were of equal importance to the party: 1) To create the illusion of mass participation; 2) To get only the right people — *i.e.*, those
trusted by and acceptable to the party — on the precinct
commissions. Besides, the area election commission, and
above it the central one, could rectify any slipups.

Once the election machinery is organized the party machinery has time to turn its attention to the next job, the nomination of candidates. It is at this point that a peculiar Soviet phrase begins to blossom on propaganda banners and in the newspapers. The illusion of a free election also requires that there be persons who are not Communist party members among the candidates, but the interests of the dictatorship demand that these non-party people be, in all other respects, completely docile to party direction. In the United States, we call such people fellow travelers, and we have seen a great many of them. They are identified by the same name in the Soviet Union, too, except at election time. Then they become members of the "bloc of Communist and non-party members." If this phrase sounds contradictory or confusing, it is purposely so. But Stalin, at the time of the 1937 election, clarified everything. He said: "The only difference is this: some are in the party and some are not."

Soviet laws provide that any enterprise such as a factory, an office staff, a military unit, or even a group of people all living in one house may nominate any candidate they choose for the Supreme Soviet. This sounds like the ultimate in democratic procedure. But, even while the election machinery is being organized, the party is busily laying the groundwork to manipulate this provision to its own interests and welfare. In any given election area, the party activists in each enterprise of any size set up small committees whose duty it is to confer with similar small committees from all the other enterprises in the area with the stated aim of agreeing on a nominee. Since the name of the nominee usually comes down from the party Central

Committee, the real purpose of these meetings is not who to put up but how to make it look good.

In the elections of 1946 there emerged two classic patterns, with some local variations. The first of these could be called the "favorite-son" type, and the second, nomination by elimination.

The nomination of Stalin, from the Stalin area of Moscow, was the best example of the favorite-son method. It was accomplished nine days before nominations closed. In the assembly shop of the Moscow Electrical Equipment Factory, the biggest Soviet enterprise in the area, 7,000 of the plant's workers were gathered on a workaday Wednesday afternoon. From the white-painted steel beams overhead, and along the whitewashed brick walls, hung big red streamers, many of them bearing this legend: "February 10, All to Vote for the Bloc of Communists and Non-Party Members." At the center of one side wall, a long table stood on a very high dias, and behind it were enormous portraits of Lenin and Stalin. Draped around them was another slogan: "Long Live the Stalinist Bloc of Communist and Non-Party Members."

At the table sat the factory party bosses, the area party bosses and a distinguished visitor from the party center — Georgi Popov. But the chairman of the meeting was the head of the factory union, a non-party member. Out of the 7,000 persons jammed into the shop he recognized one of the least significant, a slim, dark, retiring fellow in a blue serge suit who climbed up to the table and the microphone. He was identified as a mechanic named A. N. Sharov. He said: "I was born in a plain peasant family. My country, led by Comrade Stalin, gave me an education, technical training, and taught me to love my work. As a toolmaker of the seventh category, I've been working in this plant ten years. I shall continue to give unstintingly of my efforts in order that my Soviet country may become mightier still. I, a non-party skilled worker of the Moscow Electric factory, propose the candidacy of our beloved Comrade Stalin."

We are asked to assume that he was surprised at being called upon, and made his speech and choice without reflection. Anyway, the applause was thunderous. Other speakers followed — the chairman had no difficulty recognizing them from among the massed 7,000 — and to repeated thunders of approval each added a few bits of praise for Comrade Stalin and seconded his nomination. After a long period of this, the chairman observed: "I take it there are no other nominations. Therefore, nominations are closed."

From his pocket he pulled a typewritten paper and read: "The Moscow Electric factory, having discussed the question of nominating a candidate for deputy to the Soviet of the Union from the Stalin electoral area of the city of Moscow, hereby resolves to nominate the true continuer of the cause of Lenin, the wise leader of the Soviet people, the creator of the might of our homeland, the organizer and inspirer of the historic victory over fascist Germany and imperial Japan, the brilliant army leader Josef Vissarionovich Stalin." And so the meeting ended with more thunderous applause, and Stalin became the favorite-son candidate of the Stalin area of Moscow.

Naturally, no other group in the area would think of

affronting so great a man by putting up any candidate to oppose him in his own name place.

Three days later — with six days still to go before nominations legally closed — the Moscow newspapers reported that Stalin had also been nominated in many other areas of Moscow, in Kiev, Sverdlovsk, and elsewhere in all of the sixteen union republics of the Soviet Union. But, since Comrade Stalin could go on the ballot in only one place, his nomination in so many places gave the party machinery just that many chances to exercise its pattern of nomination by elimination.

The most striking sample of this cute trick was provided in Stalingrad. Stalingraders were given to understand, correctly as it turned out, that Stalin would doubtless go on the ballot in the Stalin district of Moscow. But the nominating enterprises there were determined to find a candidate of national standing commensurate with Stalingrad's heroic glory. As a result they nominated not only Stalin but all the other members of the Politburo, and Soviet Marshal Georgi Zhukov. At this point a well-directed small enterprise put up the name of the none-too-popular A. C. Chuyanov, the boss of the local party committee. It was a foregone conclusion that every one of these fifteen nominees except Chuyanov would be nominated elsewhere, as they in fact were. As a result, when the Central Committee got around to designating which districts the nominees would be elected in, the only candidate left to Stalingrad was Local Party Boss Chuyanov.

In the Soviet system nominations close thirty days before election. This not only provides time to check the list of candidates and rectify any errors which might have crept in, but it also provides time to get the polling places set up, print the ballots, and permit some electioneering.

Soviet electioneering also has a peculiar aspect. The candidates get less attention than the system does. Just as Soviet diplomats outside the Soviet Union spend most of their time accusing other nations of the crimes they know the Soviet Union to be guilty of, so within the Soviet Union more attention and space is given to proclaiming a Soviet election the world's fairest and freest than to anything else. Of course, a Soviet candidate is an office seeker without an opponent or an issue, which may account for some of it. But even when that fact is considered, the Soviet press still seems to be stretching its arms out of joint reaching for startling things to say. One paper reported that the United States was in the grip of a national problem due to young girls being forced into prostitution by unemployment; another pointed out that in thirty years many governments had fallen in the bourgeois West while the Soviet government had stood unshakeable and concluded: "In no other country can we find an example of such confidence by the people in its government, the only real people's government in the world." A third paper utilized the services of a professor of literature to prove that the works of Dickens, Mark Twain, Upton Sinclair, Stendhal, Balzac, de Maupassant, Anatole France and Romain Rolland all proved only "that the essence of bourgeois democracy consists of the preservation of those who have riches."

This theme of Soviet superiority flowered more directly, if less learnedly, in thousands of speeches at thousands of election meetings exactly as if thousands of parrots had been suddenly loosed with only one phrase on their tongues. But the parrots ranged from Politburo members down to the least important neighborhood and village supporters of the candidacies of unopposed candidates.

Consider the election meeting in behalf of Candidate Ivan Feodorovich Panin, a blond, slim, youngish party member and locomotive driver nominated to run in the Dzerzhinsky area of Moscow. The meeting hall was less than one third full, and on the stage Candidate Panin sat, looking a trifle self-conscious as he heard himself described as a peasant's son who had gone to work on the railroad while still a mere boy, but who, by diligence, perseverance, night study and his membership in the glorious party of Bolsheviks, had not only raised himself to the level of an engine driver but also to a candidacy for the Supreme Soviet. "Nowhere in the world," several supporters declaimed, "could such a thing happen except in the Soviet Union."

This theme was given an added twist by a thin, fierce-eyed woman in a ragged turtle-neck sweater. She said: "Such a meeting as this, where the electors and the candidate can come together and talk things over, is impossible under bourgeois capitalism." It remained for a boy to give the meeting its crowning touch of fantasy. His hair kept falling over his eyes, and he had obviously not yet bought his first razor but he was also obviously accustomed to making speeches. He said: "I am only seventeen, but I will be eighteen before election day and I am going to cast my vote for Candidate Panin and the party of Lenin and Stalin. I advise you to do the same." It was like a scene from George Orwell's *Animal Farm*. These people, like

Orwell's sheep, were totally unconscious of the raucous satire they created.

The artlessness and squalor of Candidate Panin's election meeting was an educational contrast to the exclusiveness and splendor of Comrade Stalin's. Stalin made one election campaign speech, on the night before the voting, and without prior announcement. It was given in the plush red and gold Bolshoy Theatre, home of the state-subsidized Moscow Opera, and admittance was by security police-approved, special ticket only. Not even the correspondents of the foreign press, who usually were informed of such things in advance, were told about it.

Comrade Stalin's speechmaking supporters mouthed the same superior platitudes that Comrade Panin's had uttered. The stage from which they spoke had a proscenium-high backdrop portrait of Stalin, and in front of it on a pedestal, a heroic-sized white plaster bust of Lenin. Sixteen red silk banners, each with the shield of one of the sixteen union republics on it, were hung around Stalin's portrait, and Lenin's bust was neck deep in "live" blossoms. In Moscow, in February, a live blossom means an honest flower — most floral decorations at that time of year are paper — and if these were in fact real, as the Moscow papers said they were, they were equal in value to the food a hundred families could eat in a year.

For all the Soviet contempt for bourgeois democratic customs, Stalin's speech was strictly in the bourgeois democratic campaign manner. He had a promise for the folks at home and a solemn warning for all those foreigners abroad. His promise was an end to bread rationing for the Russians, which he did not make good until two years later. His threat was a return to the Communist doctrine of world revolution which had, in fact, been Soviet policy for some time.

All over the Soviet Union his heavy Georgian accent was heard as he spoke. In homes, in the streets, the parks, the public squares, theatres, movie houses and even the circus, the wired loud-speakers, linked through a system of receivers to Radio Moscow, carried his voice beyond the select group in the Bolshoy Theatre to millions of Soviet citizens. His listeners knew that the reiteration of the doctrine of capitalist encirclement meant there would be no substantial improvement in their living standard for a long time, but most of them were made momentarily happy by the promise of more bread soon.

Next day was the day for "all to vote." The polling places opened at 6 A.M., which in that latitude at that season was at least a couple of hours before daylight. Most citizens preferred to get their civic duty done early. They found the voting centers beautifully prepared. There were impromptu nurseries where mammas would leave their babies while they waited in the voting queues. Or tables where papa could have a fast game of checkers while waiting for mamma to vote. Some even had small string ensembles to play soft music.

Booths into which a citizen might go to mark his ballot in privacy were shrouded with bright red bunting. But not many citizens used them. Each ballot bore only one name, and there was nothing a voter need do but mark his X, fold it across the middle and drop it in the box. By such an act the citizen registered his solidarity with the "Bloc of Communists and Non-Party Members" for all to see. Voters also remembered, from the 1937 election, that the election commissioners made little marks on the registration books by the names of those who used the booths, and some of those people subsequently had trouble with the political police. Plainly, unless a citizen wished to scratch the name on the ballot, or write some obscene jibe at Stalin, there was no need to go into the booth. Better to mark and fold the paper openly, drop it in the box and get out quickly. By noon nearly all those who could go to the polls had done so. Now the election workers, spurred by the party activists, carried the ballot boxes, and handfuls of live ballots, to the hospitals and the maternity wards, and to the rooms of the aged and crippled and sick, collecting the votes of all.

During election day morning, I wandered down the corridor of my hotel to the office of a fellow American correspondent, and found him bouncing in his chair and beating his typewriter in a transport of ecstasy. He had dug up an old statement by Stalin, left over from 1937, and he showed me what he had. It read: "Comrades, these are not really elections — this is a holiday." I was skeptical. The statement was true enough, but it did not seem possible that even the almighty Stalin could ever have let his mask slip that far. We got the original, called the translators, and quickly straightened it out. What Stalin had really said was: "Comrades, these are not merely elections — this is also a holiday." One had only to look out the window to see what he meant. Election day was Sunday — Sunday is still the day of rest for most Soviet citizens — but this was no ordinary Sunday.

The city's buildings were draped with miles of red bunting and garlanded with electric lights. On bunting-draped, rough lumber platforms in the city squares orchestras played and couples danced on the icy pavement. In some squares there were two stages, one for an orchestra and the other for wandering troupes of folk dancers, acrobats and clowns who belabored each other with noisy bladders. In the stores, counters groaned with sudden supplies of long-scarce luxury items such as chocolates, and in the dark little bars where normally nothing but ice cream could be had, beer and vodka were plentiful. As night came on, army searchlights stabbed the heavens with beams of red, purple, green and white light, and from time to time rockets exploded in the sky releasing showers of multi-colored fiery balls. All in all, it was the kind of show the Russian soul adores and never gets enough of — truly a holiday.

By Tuesday morning the papers were filled with miracles. In faraway Novosibirsk, with the temperature ten below zero, 370 voters had queued up to vote before the polls opened. In Yakutia, gallant, indomitable, patriotic horses had plowed through snow up to their bellies, hauling sled loads of voters to voting places. On ships at sea, in diplomatic posts in foreign countries, at remote border stations beyond the Arctic Circle, half around the earth from Bering Strait to the once German city of Königsberg (now Kaliningrad) 101 million Soviet citizens had voted, and 99.7 per cent of them supported the party of Lenin and Stalin. In Stalin's district of Moscow, the vote for Stalin was 101 per cent — a rather disturbing statistic which was hastily explained as being due to the fact that many voters, in their eagerness to give their approval to the leader, had come from outside the area to vote. But this was only a minor miracle. A major one was that all these votes, even including the ones cast by nomad tribes of reindeer breeders in remotest Yakutia, had been tallied, reported, tabulated and analyzed in little more than twenty-four hours. Triumphantly *Pravda* asked: "Was this not a demonstration to the whole world of the enormous superiority of Soviet Socialist democracy? Was it not true that the party of Lenin and Stalin had gained the unanimous support of the people by decades of unparalleled struggle?"

But *Pravda* itself carried part of the answer. It reported that in the Russian republic alone 420,000 voters had scratched their single-name ballots to write in the name of some person other than the bloc candidate. Considering the circumstances and the dangers involved this was a striking show of courage. It was also a statistic that could not be reconciled with that proud 99.7 per cent unanimity because 420,000 scratches represented more than .3 per cent of the total vote. The question it raised was whether, in fact, the vote had been counted at all.

Chapter V

KARL MARX argued that the development of the Communist state would produce a new breed of man — one whose sense of responsibility was so well developed and whose productive zeal was so finely tuned to his community's needs that the apparatus of state government would cease to be necessary; in brief, a society in which the "state" would wither away.

The Soviet Union, which pretends to be a Marxist state, has actually progressed in the opposite direction. Instead of diminishing, the state apparatus has grown to such a marked degree that Soviet theoreticians are sometimes as hard put to define the kind of state the Soviet Union is as outsiders have been. The result has been that Soviet thinkers indulge in a perennial guessing game the name of which, if it had a name, could be "what is it?"

Theoretician Pavel F. Yudin has defined the state as being the Red Army. But another definition which comes closer to the reality was advanced, in 1944, by Vishinsky who said: "The basis of the Lenin-Stalin theory about government lies in the welding of persuasion and coercion."

Vishinsky means that the Soviet state consists of propagandists and police. The Communist party's 6,000,000 members are all, in a lively sense, propagandists and their weapons of persuasion are words fashioned into big lies, little lies, and promises of pie in the sky. But words have largely failed, as they must always fail when the promised pie in the sky keeps on being deferred. Hence in the Soviet Union it is the rubber truncheon, the bayonet, the barbed wire of the concentration camp, and the ever-present, overshadowing fear of these things that gets the work done. Marx's new man is one who talks in whispers, keeps an eye over his shoulder and identifies himself by a number in a passport. For him, the three decades of Bolshevik rule have been an unending and seemingly endless Red Terror.

In its beginning, the Red Terror was a political weapon. Its formal name was the Cheka (a contraction of the Russian words for Extraordinary Commission to fight Counter Revolution) and it was created on December 20, 1917, or six weeks after Lenin seized power in Petrograd. Its purpose was the extermination of Lenin's political enemies, and its first chief was the ascetic Pole, Dzerzhinsky. Zinoviev, who years later became one of its most famous victims, laid down its charter in these words: "If, out of a hundred million population ten million do not want to obey the Soviets, they have to be destroyed physically." Another, lesser Bolshevik prescribed the method: "We do not wage war against individuals. We are destroying the bourgeoisie as a class. The first question to ask is 'what class do you belong to?' and the answer must determine the culprit's fate."

Swishing his iron broom with fanatical fervor Dzerzhinsky was never sickened by the blood that spattered his hands. Instead, he justified his method with these words: "The Cheka does not mete out justice. It is only a protection for the revolution and it cannot pay attention to whether some individuals might suffer from it or not. The

Cheka must have one aim only — victory — and it must triumph over the enemy even when its sword accidentally strikes some innocent heads."

After thirty years, innocent heads are still rolling.

Before Dzerzhinsky's death in 1926, the Cheka went through the first of its change of names. The new name was GPU (alphabetical symbol for State Political Control), and still later this was changed to OGPU to recognize the unification of all of the Soviet Union's political police into a centralized body. But even today, after further name changing, Russians still refer to political police as Chekists.

After Dzerzhinsky the boss Chekist was Vyacheslav Menzhinsky, and his chief assistant was Genrikh Yagoda, both of whom, Stalin was to charge years later, died of poison administered by his "enemies."

Menzhinsky remains the strangest of the police chiefs. He was fat, sleepy-eyed, slow-moving, but fully as lethal as his frail, intense predecessor. He liked mathematics, was a connoisseur of Persian art, played the piano well and wrote erotic verse. He also was shrewd and perceptive. Years before he had said: "If Lenin ever reaches power in fact, and not in imagination, he will make a mess of it. Lenin has striven for many years to adapt Marxism to his own personal use. Leninists are a clan of political gypsies, with a strong voice and a love for wielding the knout, imagining that it is their inherent right to serve as coachmen for the laboring masses." But Lenin forgave the slur, as he forgave Zaslavsky, because he recognized in the decadent, cynical Menzhinsky a knout wielder of exceptional ability. Menzhinsky's other talent was for organization.

It was under Menzhinsky that the Soviet political police

first began to assume its present shape. He killed no fewer people than Dzerzhinsky had, but he arrested more. Concentration and exile camps grew and spread, and naturally they needed an ever-growing force of police to guard and administer them. Menzhinsky added special staffs of military and civilian experts, established special detachments which in fact became a kind of army ready for internal service, set up workshops, factories and farms to produce the equipment the police needed and to provide food for both police and prisoners. Under Menzhinsky the capital of the police — that is to say the human labor over which it held power — was increasing at a prodigious rate. But Menzhinsky was often ill, especially during his last few years, and although he remained the man with the title of boss, after 1930 the real boss was Yagoda.

There was a period in Yagoda's life when this ruthless little man was the object of press and propaganda adulation second only to that accorded Stalin, largely because it was Yagoda who put the political police into the construction business on a gigantic scale. In 1929 a group of engineers who had become political prisoners dusted off an old plan to build a canal connecting Leningrad on the Baltic with Archangel on the White Sea, pointing out that it could be done very cheaply by using the labor of the prisoners. To Stalin, who had already plunged into the first of his five-year plans and had launched his collectivization program with its attendant imprisonment of the kulaks, the idea had both merit and appeal. He gave Yagoda a green light, and Yagoda, resurrecting a long-forgotten phrase by Lenin to the effect that under socialism criminals could be reformed through labor, used it to justify what became the

Soviet Union's first really spectacular exploitation of slave labor. The canal was dug by 300,000 prisoners transferred to the area from all parts of the Soviet Union. Overworked and undernourished they died like flies, but the canal was completed successfully. Amid the pumped-up joyousness with which its opening was celebrated, with slogans, banners, a holiday and dancing in the street, few Soviet people seemed to realize that they were observing one of the most savagely inhuman developments of Soviet rule. The Belomor Canal, as it is called, signified the arrival of slave labor as a permanent and important feature of the Soviet economy. This, in turn, provided a reason for the perpetual continuance of the Red Terror.

With these developments the Soviet police system assumed the shape it still retains. It has twice since changed its name, the first time in 1934 when it was reorganized into the NKVD, and again in 1946 when it became the MVD-MGB. In 1941, within the framework of the NKVD, a special branch was recognized as the NKGB, and the 1946 change-over formally recognized this NKGB as a separate ministry. What this now means is that there are two entwined ministries, both under the supervision of Politburo member Beria. One is called the Ministry of Internal Affairs (MVD) and the other the Ministry of State Security (MGB).

At the age of fifty, Georgian-born Beria displays the true stigmata of the Soviet commissar. He is slack-jowled and puffy fat — signs of a well-supplied trencherman in a hungry land. He affects a stern, unsmiling visage — proof of his serious devotion to the cause. He wears glasses — showing not only that he can read, but does. He has written a book "exposing" the Trotskyist-Bukharinist "falsification"

of history, called *To the Question of the History of Bolshevik Organizations in Transcaucasia* — which is testa-
ment that in addition to being a policeman and a scholar
he is an unswerving acolyte of Stalin, a vitally necessary
qualification.

When Beria was placed at the head of the NKVD in
1938, a good many Soviet citizens, misled by the pince-nez
and the book, raised hosannas on the assumption that Stalin
had at last decided to put his cops in the charge of a history
professor. The assumption only proved how little they
knew. All his adult life Beria had been a Chekist.

While still a student, aged eighteen, Beria became a
Bolshevik in March, 1917. Two years later the Baku Polytechnic gave him a diploma as an "architect-engineer-
constructor." Few things could have been of less use — he
had stayed on in school only because the Bolshevik party
had assigned him to organizational work among the
students.

His next assignment was quite different. In 1920 the
party, jointly with the 11th Red Army, sent him into
Georgia (reared in Sukhumi, he had a native's grasp of the
language) to organize an armed revolt against the Transcaucasian government then in power. Moscow had gone
through the hocus-pocus of recognizing this government
and exchanging diplomatic representation. But under
cover of this false friendliness Moscow was also determined
to seize the Transcaucasus for the Communists.

While thus engaged in fomenting revolt against the government of a friendly state, Beria was arrested and expelled
from the country, an armed guard escorting him across the
border. But his mission later bore fruit. A Communist in-

surrection toppled the Transcaucasian government, much as Lenin had toppled the Kerensky one, and Georgia became the Third Soviet Socialist Republic.

Beria then went back to his native Georgia as local chief of the Secret Operations division of the Cheka, and chief of the Special Services section of the Red Army. From there out, Comrade Beria's life was one zealous cop's promotion after another. By 1931, he was chief of the Georgian GPU, chief of the Transcaucasian GPU and deputy chief of the All Soviet GPU for the Transcaucasian area.

By 1935 he had received seven decorations, including the Order of Lenin, for his work in "smashing and routing anti-Soviet parties in Transcaucasia," and for his "true Leninist-Stalinist persistency in his intolerance toward the enemies of the people in the struggle for the general line of the Bolshevik party." Two of his decorations were the twice-won "Mark of an Honorable Chekist." His appointment to head the NKVD was an obvious natural.

The scope and function of the entwined organisms Beria now directs is a fantasy in proliferant iron-fisted bureaucracy. They have two major tasks: 1) to keep down political opposition; 2) make total state planning work. Taken together, they comprise not only the world's biggest police force, but also the world's biggest construction trust. The millions of prisoners kept in slave-labor camps by this police combine dig coal, gold and canals, cut timber, lay roads and railroads, build dams, factories and towns. The Soviet Union's officially estimated labor force, exclusive of agricultural workers but including clerical and professional employees, is 33,000,000 persons, a figure which takes no account of prison population. The police-directed slave-labor force is variously estimated at from nine to 30 millions. Accepting the conservative estimate of 12 million still leaves a staggering situation in which every fourth employee of the Soviet industrial apparatus is a slave worker.

It can be truly said that these men and women (every tenth prisoner is a woman) work for bread alone. Bread is their wage and death their usual reward. But even their food payments are arranged on an incentive, speed-up system. He who does the most work gets the best ration, but even the best is often not enough. The death rate, mostly from tuberculosis brought on by undernourishment and exposure, is appalling. Recently, for the third time in thirty years, the Soviet Union abolished the death penalty, substituting for it maximum punishment of twenty-five years at hard labor. Obviously there is no sense in shooting a man when he can be worked to death, but twenty-five years is sheer optimism. The life expectancy of a Soviet slave laborer is closer to ten.

Yet, even a partial list of what the MVD has created with its human capital since the completion of the Belomor Canal makes an impressive recital. It includes:

The Moscow-Volga Canal, linking Moscow by water with the Caspian Sea. This is an important artery, in peace or war, and its system of lakes and reservoirs is being stocked with hydroelectric plants; in September of 1945 the Volgastroi MVD announced completion of a 55,000-kilowatt power station on Rybinsk Reservoir north of Moscow, begun in 1937.

Along the Pechora River, in the tundra of the Komi Autonomous Area in northern Russia, MVD labor is mining lignite and oil shale and developing water power. The whole Komi area, half as big as Texas, is an MVD preserve and the president of its so-called Supreme Soviet is Gennadi Vasilievich Vetoshkin, an MVD general.

In the northern reaches of the Ural Mountains, north of Serov, formerly Nadezhdinsk, the Bogoslovski MVD is creating an industrial complex for production of aluminum, coal, iron, gold. It has built a power station, opened a two-million-tons-a-year coal cut, and is building an aluminum plant at "forced tempo." The name of Nadezhdinsk, derived from the Russian word for hope, was changed to Serov to honor MVD General Ivan Alexandrovich Serov. His name, incidentally, could have come from the Russian word for brimstone.

South of Nadezhdinsk the Tagilstroi MVD is at work. And south of that, in Chelyabinsk, the Chelyabmetalurstroi MVD is busy. This trust has reported the completion of one blast furnace, one agglomeration plant, one steam-electric power station, one rolling mill and a large repair shop.

East of the Urals, roughly along 1,200 miles of the Trans-Siberian railway, the USSR-MVD reported the construction of four hydrolysis plants, at Tavda, Kansk, Krasnoyarsk and Lobva.

Then there is the infamous Dalstroi MVD. This is a gigantic gold-mining, railroad and highway-building and port-development trust in the far northeast. Initiated in 1932, it was among the earlier of the giant MVD development trusts. Its assignment was to exploit the rich gold and platinum deposits of a vast area lying between the Kolyma and Indigirka rivers. It built its own port, now a city of 40,000 persons called Magadan, on the Sea of Okhotsk.

Nowadays, Soviet cartographers ignore Magadan when they make maps. The Soviet Union has no desire to let the world know how desperately, or at what cost, it is digging gold.

This area contains the world's coldest spot. The temperature in winter ranges from minus 30 degrees Fahrenheit to minus 90 degrees. In summer the land swarms with hungry insects who will not be denied, and though the temperature goes up to around 50 degrees, the ground never thaws more than a few feet below the surface. In its sixteen years of operation, Dalstroi has poured millions of prisoners into this area, sometimes at the rate of half a million a year. Inadequately fed, improperly clothed, shabbily housed, millions have coughed, frozen and worked to death. But the men currently in charge, MVD Lieutenant General Ivan Fyodorovich Nikishov and Engineer Colonel V.A. Tsaregradski, have been swamped with honors and decorations,* including the Order of Lenin, for "developing industry in the far north and insuring fulfillment of plans for the output of rare and nonferrous metals."

The gold thus obtained has steadily poured into the United States for the purchase of many things — locomotives, tin plate and patents. It has also bought power tubes for Radio Moscow which daily, in most of the world's languages, calls upon the workers of the world to unite and strike off their chains.

Like Nikishov and Tsaregradski, an MVD slave master named Alexei Nikolaivich Komarovski also had the gold

---

* Nikishov also won praise from Henry Agard Wallace, the Progressive who wants to be United States President. See *Soviet Asia Mission,* by H. A. Wallace.

star of Lenin's Order pinned on his chest. Radio Moscow trumpeted his paean of thanks to the world. It was: "Dear Josef Vissarionovich [Stalin]: We wish you health and strength for many years for the good of our great homeland."

In their book,* *Forced Labor in the Soviet Union,* D. J. Dallin and B. I. Nikolaevsky have identified and located 125 slave-labor camps or camp clusters (a cluster usually is made up of ten camps containing an average of 1,200 prisoners each) which stretch half around the world from Murmansk to Kamchatka.

Enormous as this operation is, it is only a part of the responsibilities of the entwined MVD-MGB. In addition, they guard the Soviet borders to keep out foreign spies and keep in potential runaways and the Iron Curtain is, in actuality, a barbed-wire fence patrolled by MGB troops and specially trained dogs. The visa of every person who enters the Soviet Union, foreigners and Soviet citizens alike, must be approved by the MGB. They also run the fire and ordinary police departments of the Soviet cities; provide the bodyguards for the Kremlin hierarchy, keep stooge-informers in every multiple dwelling, factory, mine, big office or other enterprise in the land. In many of these the MVD man is so powerful that all others call him chief.

The political police have their own research laboratories, one of which has proudly proclaimed the development of a termite-proof paper on which police records will last for 600 years. But even if, in some far-distant time, these nearly imperishable records ever come before the world's eyes, there is no assurance they will tell the whole story. As one

* Yale University Press, 1947.

Communist told Nikolaevsky: "The exact number of victims will never be found out, because those things were never counted. The task of the government is to create a new man with a new morale, according to which it will be as easy to kill on the party's orders as to drink a glass of water."

Prisoners fall into three categories: 1) criminals; 2) *bytoviks*; 3) political offenders. The word *bytovik* is derived from the Russian word *byt* which means mode of life, and a *bytovik* is usually a former state functionary who may have been anything from a factory director to a vendor of lemonade convicted of bribery, speculation, or other non-political acts which can be considered an offense against the Soviet mode of life. In the camps, the *bytoviks* usually wind up as trusties with administrative jobs — as a group they receive preferential treatment. Next in preference are the hardened criminals and the harder the better. They make brutal and effective straw bosses. The lowest of the low are the political offenders, precisely those who, in almost any other country, would not be guilty of any offense at all.

Soviet laws contain a whole series of statutes covering political offenses, but the Soviet government prefers not to air political cases in the public courts although public trials are almost always given to criminals and *bytoviks*. But by far the greatest number of prisoners are the so-called political offenders. Hence, in the Soviet Union the powers of the political police make a farce of all laws and all courts. In their capacity to deny any individual the right of public confrontation the police are above and beyond the courts, and in their power to bend the laws to suit their needs their function becomes one, not of legality but of expediency. Indeed, in 1937 the political police were assigned a definite quota of persons who had to be transported into slave-labor camps in order to meet the MVD labor needs. When it reached this point the Soviet political police ceased to be merely a police assigned to protect a minority grip upon a state; it became a big business with unlimited scope of human seizure to which every able-bodied human being represented a certain profit. And that is what it is today.

Soviet repression has proceeded in a series of waves. In Dzerzhinsky's time the enemy to be repressed and transported was composed of several classes lumped together under the term bourgeoisie. The killing and the exiling went on for some years.

Next there was the anti-kulak wave. As it had before Russian land ran red, and the stockades were so rapidly filled that new ones had to be constructed in great quantities. This lasted until well into 1934.

Then Vishinsky stepped into the picture. It was a half-lit period, a kind of twilight which some people thought presaged a new dawn of Soviet liberality and democracy. The OGPU was reconstituted, renamed the NKVD or People's Commissariat of Internal Affairs. A new law was proposed and adopted, which seemed to have the aim of making it henceforth impossible for the NKVD to by-pass the courts of public record in sending Soviet citizens to slave camps or to firing squads. But the last paragraph of this law — probably inspired and perhaps even written by Vishinsky — established an NKVD Special Council with powers as broad as the police had ever exercised but with one difference. The law made the state prosecutor a member of the

Special Council and Vishinsky was state prosecutor. Vishinsky put an end to Yagoda's pious hypocrisy about hard labor being a form of corrective education. He said: "Punishment cannot be reduced to education and let us not pretend that prisons are no different than schools."

Then Sergei Kirov, the Communist party boss of Leningrad, a rising power in the Communist hierarchy and a spokesman for the party elements which stood for liberalization of the revolution, was assassinated. It has been said that Stalin instigated the killing, but of that there is no proof. Stalin did use it, however, as the open door to another, more terrifying and more than ever repressive wave of executions and exiles.

Vishinsky's first step was still another law which empowered the police to execute, within twenty-four hours of arrest, any person accused of terrorism. The Red Terror now turned upon itself. Chief victims became party members and those who, while holding no party card, had become officials of importance. The previous repressive waves became vague half-pleasant memories to the people who survived this one. A description of what began happening in the slave camps at this time has been written by one of the lucky who survived:

"As a result of Kirov's murder, the number of prisoners increased to such an extent that there just wasn't enough room in the old camps. Construction brigades were hurriedly sent in, cutting trees and immediately building barracks for 'Kirov's murderers.'. . . The chief called us out into the yard, where we were made to line up and gave us a speech along the following lines: 'You are the enemies of the people! You have just committed an atrocious crime —

Kirov's murder. But despite all this you are now being given the chance to atone for your crimes against the Soviet state. You must redeem yourselves by heavy work, but you must be happy because the Soviet government entrusts you with the construction of a railroad that will be of tremendous importance for the glorious future of our great country — the U.S.S.R. Hurrah!.' "

Before all was over, the murderers of Kirov were numbered in the millions and riding this wave of repression Vishinsky succeeded in disposing of, not only the remaining remnants of Stalin's enemies among the Old Bolsheviki, but also of Yagoda's successor, Nikolai Yezhov, as well as a large segment of the Red Army command. The wave included most of the famous trials, in which lifelong Bolsheviks and charter members of the Bolshevik state were convicted of being Nazi agents. By 1939 the wave had spent itself — giving out largely for lack of fresh material and also because of the sudden *rapprochement* between Stalin and Hitler — but by it Vishinsky elevated himself to a place of power in the Bolshevik regime which no other Old Menshevik had ever achieved.

The next wave had to wait until war's end. This one was managed by Beria, who though no less ruthless and determined than his predecessors, used a smoother, less publicized technique. From war's end until now, the Soviet Union has repatriated more than 6,000,000 of its people from that part of Europe now in Western hands. These people had been army deserters, persons who fled from Soviet Russia at the first opportunity, and those forcibly deported for labor by the Nazi hordes. It would be a conservative statement to say that no less than half the repatriates are now in slave camps. In addition, the camps have received large numbers of former Red Army soldiers who, during the demobilization process, were discovered to have become infected with Western ideas and so were deemed dangerous. And, of course, there are the hundreds of thousands who have simply been kidnaped wherever the Red Army went — in Latvia, Lithuania, Estonia, Germany, Poland, Czechoslovakia, Rumania, Bulgaria, Yugoslavia, Hungary, Austria, and perhaps even Albania. Maintenance of slave-labor supplies seems to have become a kind of Soviet mania. Next to the firing squad it is the only method they have developed for dealing with political minorities.

As now constituted, the Soviet political police retain the power, through the Special Council created in 1934, to dispatch citizens without public hearing or public explanation. Against this salient fact, the whole system of judiciary becomes a farcical thing, because it is part of the function of a judiciary to protect a people against its own police.

But the Soviet Union does have a judicial system. It has a supreme court which consists of sixty-eight members and exercises not only a judicial function of review of lower-court decisions, but also an administrative function in overseeing the general work of the lower courts. The Supreme Court also has a Military Collegium which consists of Army and MVD officers, who try political cases. Sometimes cases are branded as political which seem, on analysis, to have no element of politics in them.

A sample was the murder of Comrade Maria Alexandrovna Belyaeva, a party member and director of a candy factory in Moscow, who was foully done to death with a blunt instrument in her office. In reporting the death of

Comrade Belyaeva the Soviet newspapers did not mention that she had been murdered. But the story of her murder skittered through the city with lightning speed. Even as isolated as a foreigner is in Moscow, I heard that she had been murdered the day her death was published. But after the report of her death, there were more than two months of silence until two Moscow newspapers carried a small item. Here it is in its entirety:

"On the 30th of January, 1947, the Military Court of the Moscow district heard the case of A.V. Adveyev, charged with committing a terroristic act against the director of the candy factory named after Babaev, a deputy to the Moscow Soviet, Comrade M.A. Belyaeva.

"In 1944, Adveyev was discharged from the factory for stealing. During 1945-46 he tried many times to get his job back, but was not accepted. Being irritated against the director of the factory, Adveyev decided to kill her and he elaborately worked out his plan. On the 20th of November, 1946, he came into the reception room of her office, waited until the visitors and employees left the room, locked the door on the inside and then rushing into her office, brutally killed Belyaeva.

"The Military Court found Adveyev guilty of committing this terroristic act and taking into consideration that the brutal murder of Belyaeva was accompanied by brutal torture, and also that the crime committed by Adveyev witnessed his special irritation against Soviet people devoted to their country and to the Communist party, sentenced Adveyev to death by hanging. The sentence has already been executed."

This little item shows two things: 1) the Military

Collegium is both a court of first instance — that is it tries cases — and also a court of last resort whose judgments are final; 2) Soviet prosecutors can classify as terrorism almost any act they choose and deal with the accused summarily.

Beneath the Supreme Court there are two layers of courts, the district courts and the people's courts. The district courts are partly appellate bodies, dealing with appeals from the decisions of the people's courts. Shortly before I left Moscow, I spent a day in one of the people's courts and the report on what I saw, heard and felt, written while it was still fresh in my mind, and subsequently killed by censors, follows:

Since what goes on in minor courts everywhere throws a revealing light on how the people live, I paid a visit to the people's court for the Sverdlov area of Moscow recently. The building, No. 27, Street of Chekhov, proved to be a two-story structure with an ornate façade which had apparently once been the private residence of a person of means. Double doors opened off the street, and in the vestibule a wall directory stated that the ground floor was given over to a complaint bureau, a record room, and a clerk's office. A broad marble staircase, down the center of which was a worn scarlet runner, led by easy flights to the second floor. At the top of the stairs, on a brown pedestal, was a plaster head of Stalin staring fiercely at all who climbed toward him.

At the top, knots of men and women were clustered around the stair well. Some betrayed inner agitation by the way they took quick, deep pulls on their cigarettes and talked in nervous, jerky snatches. But there were others who stood aloof and smoked with leisurely unconcern — casuals who had come in out of the cold for free entertainment and warmth.

There were six hearing rooms on this floor, with legal actions proceeding in four of them at once. The narrow, dark corridor which fed these chambers was lined with folding wooden benches against each wall, and on these sat more waiting litigants, lawyers and casuals.

A number of the spectators had crowded into Court-room Three. This was a room with a low, white ceiling with raised floral designs worked into the plaster, light green walls, and a large framed lithochrome of the late Soviet President, Mikhail Kalinin, hung on one wall. It hung somewhat to the right of a foot-high dais on which was a composition-topped table big enough for three persons. Behind this were three high-backed chairs, the middle one at least ten inches taller than the other two, with the shield of the Russian republic carved on each. Three judges were standing between the table and their chairs, and their height combined with that of the dais explained why Kalinin was off center. Had his picture been directly behind the bench, his whiskered countenance would have been hidden every time the judges stood up to read a sentence, as they were now doing.

The room was about fifteen by sixteen feet in size. Facing the judges, the spectators stood five and six deep, leaving hardly more than four or five feet between the front row of spectators and the dais. In that space, with a blue-uniformed policeman at his side, stood a man who had been convicted of stealing 62 copies of the newspaper *Red Star* from the premises of the publishing house. At 20 kopecks each, the newspapers were worth 12 roubles, 40 kopecks retail, or about one dollar.

The middle, or presiding, judge intoned the court's judgment in a sparse voice that was surprisingly thin for a man of his size. He was a six-footer with a massive face that was a series of plane surfaces emphasized by small, dark, deep-set eyes. He wore a brown sweater under a suit jacket of coarse material which needed pressing. He had a rash on

his jowl, and had smeared it with a white salve. His associates were women. One was white haired, with a deeply
lined face, and the other a motherly looking ash blonde of
about forty.

The prisoner was by far the best-dressed person in the
room. His blond hair had been freshly cut and his face
newly shaved. He had on a Red Army greatcoat which had
been dyed navy blue, but still had its army buttons with a
raised star and hammer and sickle stamped on each. He
stood twisting a blue serge cap, but his face suggested more
boredom than concern. There was a surprised and shocked
gasp from the spectators as the judge read out the sentence:
One year at hard labor for the theft of a dollar's worth of
newspaper. With a gesture of nonchalance, the convict
slapped his cap on his head and followed the policeman
through the spectators and out. He appeared much less
stunned than some of those who fell back to make way for
him.

I came out of this room and stood in the corridor for a
few minutes. The casuals were sampling the cases. Coming
in off the street, they would stamp the dirty snow off their
feet onto the red carpet, stand about for a few minutes to
adjust themselves to the warmth, then start shopping
around. Sidling into a hearing room, they would stand
around for a few minutes sizing up the nature of the action
in progress, then slip out and on to the next. Most of them
were more than ordinarily shabby.

At the far end of the corridor was a large, light room
containing half a dozen chairs upholstered in worn,
cracked, brown leather. I went in there to write up my notes
before some details slipped my memory. Beneath the
windows was a wide marble sill, about knee height,
stained and cracked with age and use. I put one foot on it
in order to write on my raised knee and had not written
very much when a shrill racket broke out behind me. I
turned to face a little, old woman in worn slippers with a

brown shawl wrapped around her head. Arms akimbo,
beady little eyes dancing with fury, she was giving me the
highest-pitched chewing out of my life.

The substance of it was that I was obviously a person of
no culture, or I would not be putting my foot on marble
window sills. Guiltily I took the offending foot down, but
she kept on scolding until a bystander gruffly told her to
get on about her own affairs. She slithered off down the corridor, trailing a dwindling stream of falsetto abuse until,
far down the murky hall, she hit another crescendo. This
time she had caught someone dropping cigarette ashes on
the corridor carpet which was already mussed and soggy
with melting slush. I returned to my notes.

As I finished, the old scold came back again. She climbed
first into the seat then onto one of the arms of a chair to
wind a wall clock. I laughed loudly and she twisted pre-
cariously to see what had brought that on. I pointed to her
feet and told her she also had no culture. That angered her
so that she forgot the clock, jumped down, and once more
disappeared down the hall. She was silent now, but even
her silence seemed shrill.

Like the casuals, I went shopping and found a case I
wanted to hear in a nine by twelve foot hearing room next
to No. Three. It was an occupancy case. These are civil
actions involving conflicting claims between individuals for
the right to occupy a room or an apartment. For some years
now, these cases have constituted a large portion of all
business in the people's courts. In the summer of 1945, the
unadjudicated backlog had grown so great that special
decrees were passed to give them priority over other types
of legal disputes and additional courts were created to help
clear the jammed calendars.

Throughout the Soviet Union passions inflame easily
where four walls and a roof are in jeopardy. This case was
like that. Witnesses, who take no oaths in Soviet courts,
jumped uninvited to their feet to interrupt other witnesses

with expostulations, denials or recriminations. That the
whole affair did not become bedlam was due to the per-
sonality of the presiding judge. She was a small woman in
a blue silk dress, with black hair and a face that would have
been beautiful had it not been so eloquently sad. She used
her eyes to convey her authority. They were large and
black, and her glance was level, direct, fearless. Her stare
could squelch disorder more effectively than most judges
can with banging gavel and booming voice. She was also
incredibly patient, and she put up with a certain amount of
disorder because that seemed to be one way of getting at
the facts.

Her two associates, also women, said nothing at any time.
The one on her right was a monochrome in brown — brown
withered skin, brown eyes, a brown scarf wrapped snugly
around her head with one end thrown over her shoulder
and the other tucked into a brown sweater. She looked like
a limewood carving in a peasant art shop. The other, also
in brown, had a worried face and a puckered brow — like
a housewife with budget troubles.

The litigants were relatively important and the facts, as
developed by the testimony, were these: For some time
prior to June, 1941, Comrade Malchanov, an NKVD official,
had lived with his wife and infant daughter in a room at
No. 21 *Sadovaya Triumfalnaya* (Garden of Triumph),
which is one of Moscow's better streets. Malchanov was
pleased with his quarters — he had a room fifteen by
eighteen feet with three windows overlooking the street.
However, at war's outbreak (June, 1941) Malchanov had
received orders to report for duty as commandant of security forces at Kuntsevo, a Moscow suburb in the vicinity of
the Politburo dachas, and his wife, a student engineer, went
to work in an airplane factory. They left the room. Malchanov told the "house committee" — which is what the
police stooge in every multiple dwelling is called — that he
had been called up for Red Army duty and the statement

was recorded in a thick, worn volume such as all house committees are obliged to keep. Thereafter neither Malchanov nor his wife paid any rent on their room, as they should have done if they intended to reclaim it. Now, Malchanov's job at Kuntsevo was at an end, and he had been required to give up the general's dacha he had been living in there. He wanted his old room back.

But the room had another occupant. Two months after Malchanov moved out, Comrade Chebyurov moved in. Chebyurov had been an officer in the Red Fleet, based in Leningrad, and had received an order transferring him to Moscow and the ministry of iron and steel as a technical specialist. He liked the room, too, as did his wife and three children and he wanted to keep it. He had even rigged up a partition dividing it into two rooms, and he thought this entitled him to special consideration.

The big problem in this case was one of red tape. How had Chebyurov gotten it in the first place. Had he bribed the house committee to give it to him, as so often happened? Or had it been properly assigned to him by the living space division of the Moscow Soviet, as he claimed. For, though he insisted his occupancy was legal, Chebyurov could not produce the papers to prove his contention, and said they had been lost. In any event these were the facts in the case, developed after more than two hours of testimony, which involved many interruptions.

The most impassioned and irrepressible interrupter was the wife of Malchanov. She was a big, hard-faced, aggressive woman, and at one time or another she charged: 1) her technical library which had been left in the room had disappeared, the implication being that Chebyurov had stolen and sold it; 2) Chebyurov did not work in Moscow and thus had no right to living space; 3) obviously he had obtained the room through some illegal deal with the house committee. Finally, when the evidence was in and the lawyers took over, she began to heckle them too, and kept it up until the judge threatened to have her ejected.

Four lawyers were involved in this case. The legal question that had to be argued was this: was Malchanov entitled to consideration under a decree of 1941 which extended special privileges to Red Army officers who had to give up their rooms? The same privileges had not been extended to NKVD officers until 1945, or too late to cover Malchanov's case. That, of course, was why he had told the house committee about a "Red Army" assignment in 1941. Even if he was an NKVD officer, his hands were a little soiled.

First to speak was the representative of the living space division of the Moscow Soviet. He was a tall, serious, lisping young man who said the bureau he represented felt Malchanov no longer had any right to the room. Then Malchanov's lawyer, a big, bumbling man, had his say and was, in turn, answered by Chebyurov's spokesman, a plain little woman in a red sweater and bobby socks. Last to speak was a small bald man from the public prosecutor's office. His first words were: "I wish to assure everybody that the prosecutor's office has only the friendliest feelings for the NKVD, but in this case there is the law to be considered." He then went on to say that the prosecutor's office felt that the law was against Comrade Malchanov — for whom he had only the highest personal regard — and had advised him to that effect before this action was begun. When he finished the court rose, and filed out into a back room to deliberate.

Hardly had the ladies of the bench left before Malchanov's seething wife took one long step from her seat against the wall, and towering over the hapless little prosecutor, grated at him: "From your very first words, it was plain you were against us. I am a party member, and I want you to know what is in my mind." Her husband, up to this point, had seemed a curiously insignificant sort of man.

His face was an abnormally small one, made up of abnormally large features — an enormous inverted ski slope of nose, protuberant, heavy lips and chafing-dish ears. He had given his testimony in a voice so low that it was scarcely audible three feet behind him and now, in the same unhurried, low voice, he told his wife to shut up. She collapsed back into her chair like a pricked balloon, and she stayed that way.

The judges took nearly an hour to reach a decision. While they waited, the people involved sat around muttering, or going out to the stair landing for a smoke. Malchanov's lawyer bumbled with advice to Malchanov not to take an appeal if the decision was against him. Chebyurov, a big, ruddy man with an impressively good blue cloth overcoat with astrakhan collar, sat in a corridor corner, holding his head in his hands. Once he lit a cigarette, whereat the old scold pounced on him. Then he went and stood behind a door, not in order to smoke, but merely to make himself less visible. The decision, when it was announced, was an obvious attempt to placate both sides. The judges ruled that Malchanov had no claim on the room, but they also ordered an investigation into the circumstances under which Chebyurov had obtained it. Spectators filed out muttering, "Very wise . . . very fair." They alone seemed satisfied.

It was now midafternoon, and I went case shopping again. On the opposite side of the corridor I found a room with a ceiling almost twice as high as in the other courts, and three tall windows which admitted enough daylight to make additional artificial light unnecessary. The walls were painted an electric blue, and around them above the picture molding, white plaster cherubim either floated or clung with grasshopper innocence to willowy acanthus leaves. The room was big — about twenty by twenty-four feet — and only partly filled. Here there were benches and chairs for spectators, sparsely occupied by old women with gray shawls over their heads and gray felt boots wearing through at the heels.

A single judge presided over this trial. She was young, and pretty in a well-tailored suit of good material. She wore a hint of lipstick, which none of the other women judges had worn, and her silky blonde hair was softly coiffured. Before her sat a ragged little urchin of a boy. His face was both furtive and fearful. The hinges on the door, which was at his back, needed oiling and squeaked each time the door opened. With each squeak the boy's eyes and face swung back toward the door, as if expecting some new misfortune to bear down on him.

The evidence in this case had been finished before I entered. The judge, looking down at the boy, inquired: "What do you say for yourself?" Miserably, he answered, "I won't do it again."

The judge announced there would be a few minutes' recess while she prepared sentence. I had no idea what the boy's crime was, but decided to wait. The door creaked, and another spectator from the occupancy case slid into the seat beside me. He was a youngish man, and the room fascinated him. Looking around, he remarked: "Very good. I would like to have a room like this to live in." I agreed it was a very nice room and he fell silent while his eyes hungrily pursued the plaster cherubim around the walls.

Except when the door opened, the boy sat staring at the floor before him. The threadbare overcoat which he was wearing was torn, and through the rent its brown, mottled interlining trailed like a living organ. Once he tucked his feet up on the rungs of his chair, exposing the soles of his boots. They were worn through, and curled wisps of dirty gray paper, possibly *Pravda*, protruded through the oval holes.

After about ten minutes, the judge returned and, standing at a corner of the bench, began to read from a long sheet of paper. From what she read I learned that the boy was Vladimir Shevyerev, aged sixteen, a locksmith at a Moscow brake plant and that he had been convicted of a third offense of being twenty-one minutes late to work. Reviewing the history of previous offenses, the judge recounted that on his first offense he had been reprimanded, and for his second, fined one quarter of his pay for a period of six months. For the third offense, she now ruled, he must be deprived of one quarter of his pay for nine months, which was about as lenient as the law permitted her to be.

The boy mumbled something and stood up to go. At this point the door creaked again and the old scold stuck her head in, shrilling without ceremony: "Do you want lights?" As usual, the boy had jerked his head around at the sound of the door, and the judge had seen his movement — purely animal in its quickness and palpable fear. It seemed to have startled her, in any event she did not answer. I thought: "So, the guardian of culture is also the keeper of light." The old scold shrilled again: "Not necessary." After another moment of silence she scurried off, and I did not wait to hear that door sound again. I had had enough, and while it was still open, got out.

Although all the judges I saw in action were grave, serious, and thoroughly dignified in a shabby way, Soviet judges, like all bureaucrats, do have their moments as the following item from *Pravda* (September 9, 1945) attests:

Suleimanov's beard is of recent origin. There was a time when he used to shave. His conflict with the hairdresser arose quite suddenly, not unlike a bad case of flu. What happened was that hairdresser Poleschuk dared . . . yes, indeed, dared to ask him, a People's Judge, to await his turn. This is the extent to which morals in the Budyonny district have deteriorated!

At first, the judge did not quite understand what had happened. Perhaps the hairdresser had not understood. Or, perhaps she had not recognized him. He raised his voice: "I am Suleimanov . . ." "Take a seat, Comrade Suleimanov. You will not have long to wait."

Then he understood the secret meaning of the event. He was not respected. He, a People's Judge, was put on the same footing as other clients. "You will be responsible for this, according to law," he shouted. He rushed to his room and tried — without convening court or ordering any proper investigation — the case of "the public insult by citizen Poleschuk, of People's Judge Suleimanov." The accused was sentenced to four months forced labor, but being humane the judge revised this sentence to ten days imprisonment. The hairdresser was arrested and spent two days in jail. The prosecutor intervened and she was set free.

Her first reaction was to find out whether Suleimanov had any special powers. It appeared he had none. The prosecutor of the Kirghiz Republic expressed the view that considering the scandalous violation of socialist legality, Suleimanov ought to be immediately removed from his post. For some time the Kirghizian Commissariat of Justice did not agree and did not reply to the prosecutor's office. But the hairdresser reacted in her own way, and refused to shave Suleimanov.

At last, the commissariat removed Suleimanov from the duties of judge of the Budyonny district, and transferred him to the office of People's Judge of the Kochkor district. There is a hairdressing establishment there, too.

The moral doubtless is that bureaucrats will be bureaucrats, even when they are minor judges. But it is in such hands that administration of the less stringent elements of the "coercion" Vishinsky defined as an indispensable element of Soviet power is placed.

Chapter VI

THE third pillar of Stalin's power is the Red Army.

In August of 1945, while Japan was still being fought and the grand Anglo-American-Soviet alliance still existed, General Dwight D. Eisenhower paid a visit to Moscow. His journey coincided with the season of the annual Soviet sports parade which was held in Red Square that year. The parade was a five-hour spectacle of youth from cradle age to physical maturity who, plumped and browned by two months of extra rationing and intensive training, marched, did folk dances, mass calisthenics and similar physical culture stunts in brightly colored costumes especially issued for the occasion.

As a courtesy to Eisenhower, Stalin invited him to join the Soviet political and military hierachy on the balcony of Lenin's tomb and in the course of the five-hour review remarked to the American commander that such shows were excellent for their effect on the people. "This," he said, "develops the war spirit. Your country ought to do more of it."

Two or three nights later, at a party United States Ambassador Averill Harriman gave for Eisenhower in Spaso House, the United States Embassy residence, it was announced that Japan had capitulated. Noticing that Soviet Marshal Semyon Budyonny — the Old Bolshevik with the magnificently cultivated cavalry mustache — seemed to have been dispirited by the news, Eisenhower asked him if he was not glad the war was over. Budyonny replied: "Oh, yes, but we should have kept going until we killed a lot more of those insolent Japanese." Eisenhower* comments: "The marshal seemed to be a most congenial, humane and hospitable type, but at the same time he seemed to have no concern that even one day's continuance of war meant death or wounds for additional hundreds of Russian citizens."

The juxtaposition of Stalin's remark evoked by an elaborate display of Soviet Russia's finest physical specimens, and Budyonny's indifference to their needless sacrifice for political ends, is an adroit summing up of the Soviet attitude toward the individual. But it has a particular application to the Red Army.

Individual German soldiers who fought on the eastern front in World War II have said that the thing which did most to lick their morale was not the unbearable cold, which was bad, or the too-frequent failures of supplies, which was worse, but the fact that no matter how many Soviet troops they killed more and more kept coming — seemingly inexhaustible waves of men stumbling always forward. That, too, is the Red Army. Whatever it lacks in knowledge of the science of warfare, or equipment, it makes up in numbers.

The actual size of the Red Army is the subject of a guessing game that is being carried on by the high commands of many countries. Published guesses range from two and a half million men up. My own guess is four and

---

* *Crusade in Europe.* By Dwight D. Eisenhower. Doubleday & Co., 1948.

a half million. This is based on population figures and the
fact that the Soviet Union has a universal military service
law from which exemptions are few and hard to get. At
its present population level the Soviet Union should have
between one and a half and two million young men turning age nineteen every year. Although the term of service
varies with different branches, the average is three years,
hence the number of men always in training is three times
the annual draft. On the other hand, Soviet military leaders
told Britain's Field Marshal Viscount Montgomery of
Alamein, when he visited the Soviet Union in 1946, that
the number of men in the Soviet Armed Forces was around
3,000,000. Whatever the number may be, the fact is that it
is the biggest army on the European continent — if not in
the world — and it could be put into action on a moment's
notice. Though he might not be able to keep it there, Stalin
could plant the hammer and sickle on the English Channel
any time he chose.

This fact is the one big reality in Soviet foreign policy
in Europe. It keeps European statesmen jittery and inde-
cisive and lends to that other adjunct of Soviet policy —
the native Communist party fifth columns — a sense of
power and protection. Without it they might not dare to
follow the open course of national sabotage by strikes and
other disturbances which they have been pursuing since
the promulgation of the Marshall Plan.

The maintenance of such a vast military machine would
constitute a tremendous drain on the economy of any
nation. In the Soviet Union with its poorly developed
production, its necessity of repairing war damages, and its
low standard of living, the well-being of the people is

sacrificed to the Army to a degree no genuinely democratic
people would tolerate. But, since the Soviet Union acts
upon the dictum of Clausewitz, who regarded diplomacy
as the continuation of war by other means, and vice versa,
the well-being of its people, like the lives of its soldiers, is
secondary to the accomplishment of external political aims.

Information about the Soviet Armed Forces continues to
be hazy and sketchy. In everything we read or say on the
subject one necessity remains constant. Our military
experts, both the real ones and the writing ones, woefully
underestimated it once and can do so again. But numbers
alone are not always the keys to victory — the Nazi horde
was repulsed by the Soviet Union because of many factors
of which massed man power was only one. What happened
in the Communist-Nazi clash is instructive.

In 1938, when Stalin began shooting his marshals and
generals on the pretext that they were agents of the Germans, the Red Army underwent a reorganization. Until
then it had been built on the pattern of smallish divisions—
each containing 13,000 men — with nine or more divisions
constituting an army. In the 1938 reorganization, divisional strength was upped to 18,000 men, and the system
of a corps, composed of three divisions, instituted. After
Hitler struck in 1941, the lessons of the early months caused
still another reorganization, or, rather, a reversion to the
former structure of small divisions and the abolition of the
corps. This had the effect of simplifying the chain of command which ran directly from divisional commander to
army headquarters. As before, an army consisted of nine or
more divisions and a "front" consisted sometimes of as
many as seven or eight armies. The Soviet Union was the

only participant in World War II which reorganized its forces while actually engaged in war — a terrific confirmation of prewar weakness.

The 1939-40 war with Finland had also taught some invaluable lessons. It tested the endurance of the individual soldier in winter warfare, and it dictated the provision of winter equipment in colossal quantity. At least one Soviet officer, a Major General Ignatyev, has ascribed the superiority of the Red Army over the Wehrmacht in winter warfare to four items: (1) thick felt boots; (2) skis; (3) hooded white gowns worn over the regular uniforms; (4) knowledge of how to combat frostbite by smearing the face with grease and blackening cheekbones against snow blindness.

In the first three months of the war Hitler made colossal advances. By October the Germans were before Leningrad and less than fifty miles from Moscow. In these two cities alone factories accounting for twenty-six per cent of Soviet production were concentrated. By Russian, and other sources, I have many times been told that the Germans could have taken Moscow without much additional effort. If they had, the war might well have been prolonged indefinitely. But, from German documents turned up since war's end, it appears that Hitler at this point suffered one of his fateful spasms of intuition and, over the objections of the German General Staff, ordered the transfer of the major German strength southward with the intent of cutting the Volga and isolating the Soviet capital. Thus Hitler and not the Red Army halted the drive on Moscow, and the halt gave Soviet General Georgi Zhukov time to bring up a seasoned Far Eastern army. The drive he launched in December, 1941, pushed the front before Moscow back far enough to make that city safe.

It is significant that this counteroffensive, and the one that came the following year at Stalingrad, were the decisive points of the war in Russia and that each was launched in weather so bitterly cold that the leather soles of the Wehrmacht's boots rang like metal against the ice-sheathed cobbled roads and the efficiency of the individual German soldier was halved and quartered by frozen ears, noses, fingers and feet.

By the time the battle for Stalingrad was joined, in November of 1942, the German Army was strung out on a thousand-mile front, hundreds of miles from its source of supply. Because of the assurance of Lend-Lease, the Red Army on the other hand was in a position to commit more of its supply resources to that one battle than it had theretofore dared do at any time or place.

Behind the German lines another important and often overlooked factor in the eventual German repulse was taking shape. In all history no invader from the West had ever held so much Russian land. The area was so vast that it could not be policed. The best the occupation troops could hope to do was hold the roads and railroads, and the larger cities and towns. This left vast areas for the organization, movement and concealment of Soviet guerrillas.

Contrary to some impressions, the Soviet guerrillas were not a spontaneous movement. The Communist party had learned a great deal about the art of guerrilla warfare in Lenin's civil war. Local Communist party leaders who fled ahead of the German army were parachuted back into localities where they were known. Other Communists who had gone underground with the German occupation were dropped necessary items of equipment, of which the most vital were radio transmitters and receivers.

The skeletal guerrilla commands received substantial reinforcements from Soviet citizens in the cities and towns which had been inundated by the German wave. At first many of them had been indifferent. Never having been happy with the kind of rule the Communist party gave them, they were ready to find out what Berlin would offer. Berlin could never hope to win actual support from these people, but it could have immobilized them by humane treatment. Instead, the occupying Nazis launched a program of racial and political extermination, and sent in the lowest dregs of German brutality to carry it out. People of the occupied areas developed a preference for the Soviet rule they had never liked and many of them translated the preference into action by joining the guerrillas.

It is a curious but inescapable fact that the shrewdest occupation policies were those of the Rumanians in the southern Ukraine. What they did was to leave the Jews alone, and attack the Soviet system at its most vulnerable point. They reestablished a measure of free enterprise, giving skilled artisans a chance to run their own shops and small factories, and set up a system of payments for farm produce direct to the producer. Now, even after five years of Soviet re-establishment in the area the people's memory of life under the Rumanians is still making trouble for the local Communist leaders.

With growth in numbers, the guerrillas became a real striking force. They supplied themselves by small, frequent raids on German stores. They developed great ingenuity in

mining supply trains. The technique was to plant mines
that would blow up the locomotives, shoot it out with the
guards, loot the trains, then vanish into the forests. Deep
behind the German front lines, they cleared and used airplane landing fields for communications with Moscow. In
forest dugouts they set up small foundries and machine
shops for the conversion of German ammunition or the
manufacture of crude but useful weapons such as small
mortars and cannon. They even had their own travelling
propagandists and agitators.

In the Partisan museum in Minsk there are hundreds of
copies of guerrilla newspapers, about the size of throw-
aways, which were printed in the forests by travelling
propagandists. Type was carried in a special vest worn
under the outer clothing. The vest had a separate pocket
for each letter so that when a man put one on he became, in
effect, a perambulating type case. Chases were crudely
made of wood, for lightness, and the rollers, about the size
of an ordinary typewriter platen, became effective only
when a man bore down hard. But with this simple equipment stuffed about his person, and a few sheets of paper,
a man could set up a print shop in any dugout he happened
to dive into.

In the area around Minsk alone, the guerrilla army
reached the staggering size of 350,000 effective male and
female troops. For safety's sake they worked in small bands,
maintained contact with other groups by portable radios,
coordinated their raids in accordance with orders from a
guerrilla headquarters and were capable, as they once
proved, of cutting a rail line in a thousand places within
a single hour. Also coordinated, through Moscow, with the

Red Army high command, they were in fact a part of the Soviet armed forces and as such played a tremendously important role in the Soviet repulse of the Germans.

Very little opportunity for observation of the Red Army in action was ever given foreigners — even the Allied foreigners. War-toughened correspondents, who had been shot at on many another front, sat in Moscow and drank themselves jittery from frustration while Soviet officials blandly ignored their requests for trips to the fighting lines, or refused them on the ground that the front was a very dangerous place. Much the same thing happened to the official military observers. Hence not a great deal of reliable information about the Red Army was ever gathered.

Certain facts, however, stand out. Artillery, always a favorite Russian arm, was plentiful and good. In this field the Red Army produced its only new weapon, the Katyusha, or rocket gun. Actually the gun was a launching platform which faintly resembled a chicken crate on which up to a dozen rockets could be stacked. The platform could be adjusted for elevation and direction and mounted on an ordinary one or two and a half ton truck. The rockets were fired in salvos, usually four or six at a time.

The Russian Navy, except for a certain amount of convoy protection on the northern supply route to Archangel and Murmansk, proved to be negligible in contrast to that of either the United States or Britain. Lately, we have been hearing a great deal about the Soviet Union now being in possession of more than 200 submarines, many of them snorkel equipped, but these reports should be heavily discounted. The Soviet production is not yet up to the task of pushing arms production on all fronts at once, and the concentration at the present is on the atom bomb and the airplane. In late 1946 I flew over the Black Sea shipyard at Nikolayev, and it was then still a useless mess of sunken ships, twisted rusting cranes and gutted shipways, just as the Germans had left it two and a half years before.

The Soviet air arm was designed, and served, more as a ground cooperation force than as an offensive fighting arm. Rocket-firing fighter planes were used as antitank weapons and the Soviet air force consisted principally of one competent but unexceptional single-engined fighter and one similarly competent and similarly unexceptional twin-engined light bomber. Under Lend-Lease the Soviet Union received from the United States upward of 5,000 airplanes of many types including Airacobra fighters, medium bombers, the versatile Douglas A-20 and the Douglas DC-3. They had no long-range strategic bombing force, no bomb sight comparable to those developed in the United States, no radar, and no ground cooperation equipment for blind flying. During the war they sequestered three American B-29s which had flown into Siberia after bombing raids on Japan. But if these ships have been copied on any extensive scale, no evidence of mass production has yet developed.

Immediately after war's end, Russian designers made Soviet headlines with predictions of new civil transport ships to come. That was four years ago, and none of them have yet appeared. The Soviet air transport for civilian use is still the twin-engined DC-3, which is also built in the Soviet Union, and is still a bucket-seat job. Soviet pilots are renowned for their dash and skill, and they do get away with chances no American civilian transport pilot would take. Because the newspapers never print a line about any Soviet air accident, a legend has grown up to the effect that Russian pilots are so skillful they never have them. This I am able to deny. In a wood near Moscow, once, I came upon the remains of a DC-3 which had been so thoroughly burned that most of its aluminum skin fabric and struts were melted into fist-sized, dumpling-shaped chunks.

Soviet pilots, like those of World War I, still must fly by the seat of their pants and the hands of their watch. Whatever may be said for this kind of flying by some people, it is not healthy.

One sample of what it can be like involved Secretary of State James Byrnes. On the one occasion he flew into Moscow, in a four-motored United States Army plane, the pilot, as all American pilots flying into Russia must, took on a Red Army navigator and a Red Army radioman in Berlin. The flight plan was simple, as the Soviet navigator traced it on a map. Flying eastward, the plane was to turn northeast when it came to a certain railroad line which the Red Army man marked. They came to the rail line and turned northeast. Fifteen minutes later they should have been over the heart of Moscow. But half an hour later they were still flying northeast and still no Moscow. More than that it was beginning to get late, and only about half an hour of daylight was left. The pilot began stooging around, seeking Moscow.

While this was going on Byrnes lost some of his *savoir-faire*. "I don't like this," he complained. "This man might hit a mountain."

"Don't worry about that," a companion assured him. "There are no mountains around here."

"Why man," Byrnes ejaculated, "the hell of it is, you don't know where here is."

Shortly afterward the navigator's error became apparent. The plane had already been northeast of Moscow when it turned northeast to follow the railroad. By turning around and following the same railroad southwest, they found the target. And just in time — it was pitch dark within five minutes after the landing.

The Soviet Union has gone in heavily for jet-propelled warplanes. In the period between August, 1946, and May, 1947, they produced at least 103 of these planes and perhaps many more. And doubtless they have gone on producing. But in any real test the problem of how they will make out with jet-propelled aircraft manned by contact-flying pilots is something for the experts to ponder.

The Soviet Union began its war with Germany in possession of a 34-ton tank called the Voroshilov. It mounted a rifle of approximately 75-millimeter calibre, and was thus deficient in range and effectiveness against the German tanks with 88-millimeter guns. It ended the war with a 60-ton Stalin tank mounting a rifle of about 105 millimeters. I know nothing about the gun's range, rate of fire, muzzle velocity or such technical points, but I'm told that it is still the largest tank-mounted gun in the arsenal of any nation.

From all this, however, it will be plain that in the Soviet Union's war with Germany many factors played a favoring part in behalf of the Red Army. The Germans were handicapped by overextension, improper equipment for sub-zero warfare, Hitler's mistakes, a stupid occupation policy, and the effectiveness of the Soviet guerrillas. Any government, or army, that ever undertakes an invasion of Russia should remember these things. Hitler could have learned many useful lessons by analyzing the circumstances which enabled Peter the Great to crush Charles XII of Sweden at Poltava in 1709.

It is clear that when Soviet Marshal Klementy Voroshilov declaimed, as he did, to the Communist Congress in Moscow in 1939, "Comrades, our army is invincible," he really meant to say, "Comrades, Russia is an awful big place." History and the facts bear out the second, but the first is still a question mark.

The Red Army consists of a permanent officer class and an annual conscription. The amount of time a conscript spends in training depends on the branch to which he is assigned, or elects to serve in. In the infantry, training lasts twenty months, in the artillery, two years; in the MVD, two years and four months; in the security police or border guard, three years, and a similar term is demanded of men who get in the tank corps. The air force demands four years to complete training.

Coupled with these differentials in service terms, there is also a differential in pay. An infantryman gets nine roubles a month, or less than the price of a pack of cigarettes. If he can qualify as an infantry chauffeur, he not only doubles his pay, but also gets a chance to hang around the homes and clubs of the top brass which usually means additional dividends in bread, sausage, vodka, cigarettes and other good things of life. In contrast to the infantryman's nine roubles, the common recruit in the MVD troops gets nineteen. Recruits to the tank corps and the air force are treated even better.

In the Red Army, lieutenants come in three categories. There is a junior lieutenant, a lieutenant, and a senior lieutenant. The junior is a kind of top sergeant, but he is a commissioned officer and his pay begins at 625 roubles monthly which is nearly one-third higher than the wage of the average Soviet employee. From there it goes up by stages to heights which are, in the Soviet economy, somewhat dizzy.

Pay is not the only incentive the Soviet officer class holds out to the Soviet boy. It is a singular but instructive fact that when Moscow determined to entertain the Foreign Ministers conference in the spring of 1947, Molotov had to study the town to find a suitable site — one comparable to the quarters provided in London or Paris — in which to hold the meetings. The choice finally fell on a club for officers of the Red Army air force. It was a plush joint on the Leningrad Road, built in the grand manner, with marble stairways, heroic-sized rooms with still more heroic-sized crystal chandeliers, walls festooned with "liberated" art treasures from European galleries and carpets which, though a little frayed in mid tread, still boasted noble selvedges. The liberated art was removed temporarily to avoid arched eyebrows, the worn parts of the carpets were simply covered over with runners from such well-known Soviet rug-production centers as Bokhara, and the foreign ministers swept wonderingly in.

The joke was only a small one, but there was a joke. Before the revolution this palace had been, not the home of a nobleman, but one of Moscow's more renowned honky-tonks. It was called the Yar, and generations of young Muscovites had sung:

> Oh, sweetheart, don't go to the Yar,
> Don't waste your money that way,
> It's better to buy a guitar
> And play on it all day.

By these and other privileges, such as special stores with special prices, and discounts of twenty-five per cent on prices in other stores, the Soviet officer is not only encouraged to think well of himself and his station in the Soviet society, he is also virtually isolated among his own kind. And, although common soldiers have the right to prefer charges against their officers when they think circumstances warrant, the officers have the more overwhelming right to shoot common soldiers out of hand when they think discipline requires it.

The privileges and prerogatives that go with the status of officer in the Red Army, however, are not easily won. There is a regulation which says that Red Army officers must have done a term of service in the ranks, but the extent to which this is actually followed is an open question. The youngest major general in the Red Army today is a twenty-eight-year-old air force officer whose name, by the strange coincidence of birth, is Vasily Stalin. He is Stalin's son.

However, the Soviet Union does strain to increase its officer class. According to Voroshilov's 1939 speech there are "sixty-three schools for land troops in which tens of thousands of splendid Soviet young men are studying and which annually turn over to the army thousands of well-trained and politically educated young officers — lieutenants — devoted to the party of Lenin and Stalin.

"Our aviation personnel," he continued, "is reinforced from the graduates of thirty-two flying schools and aeronautical engineering schools. The party and the Young Communist League supply over 20,000 of their finest members to these schools where they study to be future Red pilots, navigators and aeronautical experts. The students in these aviation schools, as well as of the other military schools, in addition to their special curricula, take a course in social and political subjects.

"But in addition to these the Red Army needs, and in large numbers at that, commanders and various highly skilled experts with university education. For this purpose the Red Army has fourteen military academies and six military faculties in civil universities which together accommodate well over 20,000 commanders, political workers, engineers, surgeons and others."

If Voroshilov was accurate in 1939, the number is probably greater now than then. His repeated mention of political workers, however, points a specialty of the Red Army.

Probably no army in history has been subjected to such intensive political education as goes on interminably in the Red Army, and in all its branches. Early in the war, it was announced that the political commissar had been abolished. As is so often true the announcement was a half-truth. The title was abolished, but the commissar stayed on — with the new title of political vice-commander. The result is that the Red Army still has its system of political control and every commanding officer from the marshal in charge of a "front" to the *polkovnik* in charge of a regiment has his political shadow with large unspecified powers and, more often than not, a more direct line to the Kremlin than the military commander has.

Among the common soldiers, the minions of this system of political overseers are called "polytrooks." According to the labor newspaper *Trud* their main duties are "concerned with carrying on agitational and organizational work among the troops and keeping them informed of party slogans, directives of the party, and the orders of their commanders. The main part of the internal party work consists in checking on the ideological development of Communists, bringing new members into the party, strengthening of party and military discipline and in leadership of party and Komsomol (Young Communist League) organizations."

Sometimes the polytrooks get fancy and one result was reported in *Red Star:* "The dugout is decorated in a manner conducive to cultured rest. It has portraits of Stalin in his marshal's uniform, members of the Politburo, the marshals of the Soviet Union and Heroes of Socialist Labor. On the walls are a big map and texts of the military oath and the new national anthem. The officers and men gladly come here to listen to lectures, reports, talks or simply rest. The activists who run the dugout arrange frequent visits by men who have distinguished themselves in battle. There is a cult of heroism."

In contrast to this cult of heroism there was a cry of anguish in *Red Fleet:* "It is necessary to appoint special party organizers to any group of men who are sent away from their unit on special assignment, such as receiving airplanes. The necessity for this was not realized until one

Communist disgraced himself while away on one of these missions."

The disgrace was not specified, but the only points at which Soviet fliers picked up airplanes were Alaska and Great Falls, Montana, both within the territorial boundaries of the United States. Could it have been that this noble Communist was traduced by the fleshpots of the bourgeoisie?

This system of politics entwined among the military can trip the ablest of Soviet soldiers. When Eisenhower stood alongside Stalin he said to Russia's Number One: "Marshal Zhukov and I get along splendidly. This is because great and powerful countries like yours and mine can afford to give their proconsuls in the field a sufficient authority to achieve accord in local details and administrative matters. . . ."

When he said this Eisenhower was only trying to put in a good word with the Boss in behalf of his friend Zhukov, a great soldier and a Russian patriot.

The background was an incident in Berlin. One day Zhukov called Eisenhower and said, in effect, "We've got a job over here and my boys don't seem to know how to cope with it. Can you send over some of your technicians and get a power plant going?" Eisenhower responded to the effect that some of his experts would be there in half an hour. Zhukov, in some surprise, said: "You mean you can do a thing like that without consulting your government?" and Eisenhower replied: "Sure, can't you? If I started consulting my government on matters like that, they'd very soon call me home and send someone else to do my job."

But the effect on Stalin of Eisenhower's statement was quite different from the one the General meant to create. Sometime afterward, Zhukov was called home on the pretext of being made chief of staff, and shortly after that he was demoted to the regional command of Odessa. Before he left Moscow, he briefly told a friend or two that he was glad to get the demotion because he was "tired of political generals."

It is doubtful if Zhukov will succeed in escaping political generals, even in secondary Odessa. When Stalin relinquished his post as Minister of Soviet Armed Forces — a job in which is centralized both the military and political command of all Soviet arms — he gave it to Politburo alternate Bulganin, a civilian in marshal's uniform. Bulganin and Zhukov knew each other well. In the days when Zhukov was battering at the Germans with many armies under his command, Bulganin was his political vice-commander. Subsequently, in another shift, a professional soldier, Marshal Alexei M. Vassilevsky, became Minister but Bulganin retained the political command.

Chapter VII

THE Communist philosophy is wholly materialistic. It denies the existence of God or a hereafter and affirms that man's paradise must be made on earth. It denies the validity of man's individual freedom, and requires each man to subordinate his own spirit to the will of the state. To compensate for these dispiriting deprivations, it holds out the promise of "security," or an economic equivalent of more pay for less work. In the Soviet Union, after thirty years of Communist party rule, the promise of a better life remains unfulfilled, and security an illusion. For most Soviet citizens, the best the economy can offer is a bleak and bitter scrabble for existence.

By dictionary definition, the word economy means the practical aspects of the production and distribution of a nation's wealth, and the level of the material prosperity of its people. Among the great nations of the Western world there are none in which production is as inefficient or distribution as inept as in the Soviet Union, and in none does so large a proportion of the population live so near the border line of starvation.

Surprisingly, even Communist propagandists and apologists will quite often admit that, in caring for the wants and needs of its people, the Soviet economy has turned in an incredibly poor performance. But they always seek to absolve the system by laying responsibility on the "backward" conditions of pre-revolutionary Russia. In doing so they throw together a jumble of figures, quotations, observations from travelers' reports and imaginary situations to paint a picture of Russian backwardness that is more nearly true of the Russia of 1870, or an even earlier time, than of 1913, the last peaceful year before the Bolshevik coup. By making Russia of 1913 appear to be much more backward than it actually was, the Communists give themselves credit for a great deal more than they have actually accomplished.

The introduction of substantial industrialization was long delayed by many factors, chief among them the institution of serfdom. But after the serfs were freed, in 1863, industrial progress gathered speed and it continued up to World War I at a constantly accelerating rate.

In its main lines, industrialization followed patterns that were familiar in the United States and in Great Britain. Trade unions were at first forbidden and later continued to be hampered by severely restrictive laws, but despite these repressions, conflicts between labor and capital arose, and labor achieved substantial gains. Along with these, there were gains for all the people. A law requiring universal education was adopted. The principal of local and national representative government not only was recognized, but made considerable progress.

In some respects the period between 1870 and 1910 was the nearest approach to an era of greatness that Russia has ever known. It produced writers like Leo Tolstoy and Anton Chekhov — forever secure among the world's greats. It also produced scientists of world renown and leadership, men who made large contributions to the increase of knowledge. Russia's greatest painter, Ilya Repin, was also one of its products. The printing industry grew prodigiously; Russian composers flooded the world's concert halls with Russian music; under Stanislavsky, the Moscow Art Theatre gained world renown. Villages grew into cities, and Moscow rapidly changed from a sprawling commercial town into a bustling industrial metropolis. Over all this change and bustle there was a spirit which clamored insistently for freer enterprise, political equality, greater individual opportunity, greater scope and rewards for the individual — for the things, in short, upon which the United States was built. Lenin himself recognized it when he explained the failure of his party of Bolsheviks to enlist a mass following by saying that "Russia was at that time the most petty bourgeois of all the big European countries." If any phrase in Lenin's vocabulary fits the United States both past and present, it is "petty bourgeois."

Though unintentionally, the official Communist *History of the Civil War in the USSR* throws a revealing light on how some workers lived in pre-Communist Russia: "The Byeloretsk Works was . . . the biggest and politically the most backward [*i.e.,* anti-Bolshevik] plant in the South Urals; 30,000 workers lived in these backwoods surrounded by lofty mountains, remote from the railway and large centers. The plant itself was the center of the Byeloretsk-Kamarov area and 11 other factories came within the radius of its influence. *All the workers in the plant owned plots of land and their own houses.*"

The mere ownership of a plot of land with a house on it creates a type of citizen whose indirect contributions to his community and his nation are enormous. With ownership goes a certain individual pride — a desire to make his house as attractive on the outside and as comfortable inside as his own pocketbook and the general community level will permit. The possession of real property gives him a real stake in the community, for the higher the community level rises the greater becomes the variety of satisfactions that enter his life. He will support schools and hospitals because he wants their services for himself and his children. He believes in clean streets, pleasant parks, law-abiding behavior and many other things, all of which add up to his being a cooperative contributor to the welfare of the community. In all of this activity he retains a sense of individuality, betokened by his home ownership. And a part of his attitude is based on his desire to enhance the value of his property. The profit motive is thus inextricably woven into the fabric of community responsibility and communal pride. Sometimes without even being aware of it, the individual homeowner perceives that human freedoms and economic freedoms are two indissoluble parts of the same thing. By instinct as often as by rational thinking, this individual bases his political decisions upon their foreseeable economic consequences.

I do not wish to be understood as saying that Russia, in 1913, had reached this level of development on anything that could be called a national or general scale. But it did represent the national trend, and it had, by Lenin's own confession, already embraced a large segment of the population. Its development inevitably contributed to the overthrow of the monarchy. Lenin clearly understood that its continued development would be as inimical to the Communists as to the Czars, and hence decreed the liquidation of the bourgeoisie as a class.

The abolition of the bourgeoisie is an indispensable element in the imposition of the Communist party system of government. It has inevitably followed wherever the Communists have seized power, and it must follow any future extensions.

Thus, United States citizens need to know how a Communist defines the bourgeoisie. In the United States it is a class which embraces not only the ultra-rich and ultra-successful — the Rockefellers, Morgans, duPonts, Fords, Chryslers, *et al.* — but the little operators whose collective face is Main Street. The men who own and run Main Street's banks, hardware stores, appliance shops, haberdasheries, grocery stores, automobile agencies, feed stores, coal and lumber yards, filling stations, and undertaking parlors are as much a part of the bourgeoisie as those who run American Telephone and Telegraph, General Motors, or Standard Oil. In the Communist view the bourgeoisie and the home-owning class are virtually indistinguishable.

In any nation, and it was as true of Russia in 1917 as it would be of the United States today, when all these people are wiped out by peremptory execution, imprisonment, or expropriation and exile, the economy suffers a deadly setback. As the state takes over everything, the large and small entrepreneurs are replaced by political appointees whose principal, and often sole, qualification is real or pretended loyalty to the party seizing power. The national system of production and distribution passes into the hands of bureaucrats. Ignorance replaces know-how, inertia succeeds initiative, individualism and incentive are abolished.

Even in Moscow, the show case of the Communist party

system, the results are so palpable as to be almost inescapable to the open-eyed visitor. While I lived in Moscow, I acquired a profusely illustrated ten-volume book on the city's growth, from its founding in 1147 through 1910. Studying photographs of street scenes, markets, shopping streets, and other such things, taken between 1900 and 1910, and comparing them with the modern Moscow after thirty years of Communist rule, I was struck not so much by the changes that had taken place as by the things which remained unchanged except through deterioration. Ordinary people were not as shabby then as now, and more people were well and fashionably dressed. The streetcars that clanged and rattled through Moscow streets in 1910 were still clanging and rattling there in 1947.

Against the propaganda boasts of colossal construction projects carried out by triumphant Communists, the actual accomplishments were strikingly meagre. Some streets had been widened, some new buildings had gone up, and a subway had been tunneled beneath the city. But, although Moscow had grown from a city of about 1,500,000 in 1917 to about 7,000,000 in 1947, it was still a startling fact that more of the city's dwelling space, and more of its schools, hospitals, theatres, railway stations and hotels had been constructed before the revolution than since. In my two years there, I saw only one new structure rise. It was a block-square, six-story addition to dread Lubianka Prison, constructed for the MVD by German prisoners of war.

Deterioration was even more striking. In Moscow, whenever one turned away from the few show streets, or the comparative handful of new, shiny buildings, one plunged precipitately into slums. The roughly cobbled streets had been ruined by years of freeze and thaw. Sidewalks were heaved, broken and lethal after dark. The doorways of the houses were dark and fetid, and through cardboard-patched windows one could see rooms lighted by a single yellow electric bulb suspended from the ceiling. The exteriors of the houses were blotched by rotting, unpainted wood, or great holes where the plaster had fallen away exposing disintegrating lathing. These things were true, not of one street, or a group of streets in one section, but all over the city.

It took neither special knowledge nor inquiry to see that streets, sidewalks and houses were all of pre-revolutionary construction. In fact, the window frames on many of the houses emphasized this. In times past, Russians delighted in decorating their houses with fancy window frames, wonderful samples of intricate scroll carving. Seldom did two houses have frames that were identical. Now, though the frames are often broken and decayed in unpainted neglect, they are a reminder that once upon a time these houses were owned by people of comparatively simple means to whom the choice of a unique frame was the expression of proud individuality.

The economics of the Communist system has discouraged possessive pride as relentlessly as its politics has suppressed individualism. Although Soviet law does not prohibit a man from owning his own house, on a plot leased from the government for a long term, home ownership is beyond the reach of all but the bigger big shots. When the ordinary citizen wants a place to live, he must apply to a bureau. Some housing is controlled by factories or other such enterprises and restricted to the employees of the given undertaking. Some is similarly controlled and managed by governmental ministries, such as the Red Army, the MVD-MGB, etc. But a large portion of urban housing is administered by housing divisions of the city or town government, called the local soviet.

Unless he is successful in bribing a bureaucrat, or well enough connected to demand favoritism, the ordinary citizen has little or nothing to say about where he will live. He takes what is assigned to him, and makes the most of it. Nor does he, if he is an urban dweller, get a whole house for himself and his family. Instead he gets a room, and sometimes it is a pretty small room. Often as many as forty to fifty people occupy one six-room house. When people must cook, eat, sleep, make love, bear children, quarrel, be sick and die all in the explicit presence of parents, siblings or offspring confined within four narrow walls, there is not much spirit left over for pride in the pretty things of life. Just staying alive is trouble enough; the average citizen is thankful that leaky roofs, cracked masonry, broken sidewalks and roller-coaster streets are someone else's responsibility.

Maintenance is the responsibility of the political, ministerial or enterprise housing division — in short, it is in the hands of bureaucrats who do not repair the house they do not live in. The things that are common to such a system are far worse than the worst aspects of the landlord-tenant system. As a sample of how top-heavy a bureaucracy-in-charge-of-housing can become, and of how it works and does not work, the following plaintive item from a Moscow newspaper called *Moskovsky Bolshevik* is illuminating:

Comrade S. Eldarov, the head of the first dwelling administration in the Rostok district [of Moscow], loves eyewash. At a recent session of the dwelling house commission of the executive committee of the Moscow Soviet, he said that capital repairs had been effected at six large houses and everything was in perfect order. A sanitary inspector thereupon told him that the water supply and the drainage system is not now working in any of the houses and their repair had not even been begun. The sanitary inspector was right.

A recent report of the administrative inspectorate of the executive committee said that repairs in the Rostok district were proceeding unsatisfactorily. The houses are in bad condition. On one street eighty per cent have leaky roofs. The water pipes are not in repair. The root of the trouble is that if a dwelling house administration spends all the money assigned to it, it is considered to have fulfilled its plan. Nobody inquires what has happened to the money, still less often whether the work is of good quality. This enables Comrade Eldarov to charge up as repairs the cost of pumping water out of a flooded cellar.

One house was charged * for the repair of 800 square yards of roof. Actually, the house has only 600 square yards of roof, and of these only 25 were repaired. In another house they simply charged up repairs without doing any repairs whatever. These frauds are known to the district soviet, which, however, has taken the culprits under its wing.

Bureaucratically speaking, the situation disclosed by this item is typical. To a "dwelling administration," a "dwelling house commission" and an "administrative

---

* This does not mean the tenants had to pay. It represents a bookkeeping transfer, the charge being made by the repair division against the rent-collecting division.

inspectorate" already busily engaged in getting no repairs done, it is proposed to add an inspectorate to inspect the fulfillment, or non-fulfillment, of plan by the dwelling administration which the dwelling house commission and the administrative inspectorate seem incapable of activating. Meanwhile the houses keep on rotting, the people become more and more miserable, and the propagandists boast that in the glorious Soviet Union rents are cheap. They should be. In most American cities the operation of sanitary codes would prohibit human beings from living in such houses at any rental.

But another question arises. Which is the more backward system, the repressive monarchy under which these houses got built, or the even more repressive Communist one under which they are crumbling away?

There is testimony on this point. In 1947 six recognized American economists, after an exhaustive study of all available data, jointly published in the *Harvard Review of Economic Studies* their conclusion that not until 1934 did the Soviet Union's production and national income return to the 1913 levels, and that in 1940 it stood at 50 per cent above 1913. Now (1949), because of the war, it is not yet back to its 1940 level. There is little doubt but that the rate of growth which obtained between 1900 and 1913, if it had been continued as it most likely would have been had Lenin not intervened, would by now have given the Russian people a far higher living scale than they have.

More specifically enlightening, however, is Victor Kravchenko's father, a pre-revolutionary member of the Russian working class, whom Kravchenko has quoted as saying to his then Communist son who had been defending the Communist regime: "Bitya, why must you fool yourself? Do you recall your life at home when you were a boy? We were not wealthy, but we never lacked for bread and milk and ordinary clothes. You and your brothers even had a nurse. We lived decently. Looking back, our existence seems almost luxurious by contrast with the life of the working class family today. Only a very small minority in the past lived the kind of starved and hopeless lives now lived by the majority. . . ."*

Twice during the time I was in Russia, I was invited to dinner in a Russian home. My first host was a person of some privilege. He had received his living quarters in a Red Army development reserved for the ranks of colonel and up.

This development was a collection of two-story houses each originally divided into four four-room apartments. Each of these apartments had subsequently been divided again into two-room apartments with a communal foyer and a communal kitchen. The settlement was approximately fifty minutes by available transportation from the center of Moscow. One rode to the end of one of the subway lines, took a trolley for an additional twenty minutes, and after that walked approximately half a mile.

The dwellings, completed in 1937, had been laid out with an evident intention of landscaping, but no landscaping had been done. Beyond the end of the trolley line the road was unpaved. My friend's family consisted of himself, his wife, two daughters aged nine and twelve. Both he and his wife worked and they had an old woman, I judged her to

---

* *I Chose Freedom*. By Victor Kravchenko. Garden City Publishing Co., Inc. 1947.

be past seventy, to do housework. She had been retired but her retirement pension was 115 roubles a month, or not enough to buy food. She therefore continued to work in order to eat, and that was the only salary my friend paid her. She slept in their home.

Each of the two rooms these five people shared was a combination sleeping and living room. The children slept together on a three-quarter bed in one room in which the old woman also had her cot, and another three-quarter bed for my friend and his wife was in the other room. Just off the foyer was a small water closet which was just that. There was a sink in the kitchen, but this house did have the advantage of running water. Many Moscow rooms did not.

We ate at a little square table about the size of a card table in the room which was also the bedroom of my friend and his wife. We began the meal with a bottle of vodka and big plates of a steaming thick soup of meat-stock base, but almost solid with noodles, chopped carrots, chopped onions, and chopped cabbage. It was good. It was followed by some sort of nondescript meat surrounded by boiled potatoes. To judge by the exclamations of the children, this was a treat — quite rare. For dessert we had some pieces of chocolate which I had brought along and which again the children found extremely delightful.

After the girls went to bed my friend, his wife and I continued to sit at the table and talk. My friend had had a number of important foreign assignments and had spent several years in the United States. In fact, one of his two children had been born in New York's Bellevue Hospital, and twelve years later his wife had not ceased to marvel

at the excellent attention she had received free of charge
in the United States.

The conversation was lively and interesting and we
drank a good deal of vodka. We also lost track of time and
did not realize until it was too late that I had stayed past the
time when the subway stopped. There was no way for me
to get back to my hotel. Quite without my realizing what
was being done, they gave me their bed and said they
would find a place in the next room. Not until the next
morning, when I had a look at that room, did I realize they
must have slept on the floor.

I awoke rather late. My friend had gone to work. His
wife, however, was still there; so was the old servant and
one of the two daughters. I had the, odd to me, experience
of waking up in a room which contained three comparatively strange females and realizing that although I was
wearing only a pair of shorts I was not going to be able to
get out of that bed unless I came out as I was in their
presence. It took a few minutes for me to get up my courage.
I arose, put on my clothes and in the process realized that
I was the only person in the room who was in the least
embarrassed. The three onlookers were completely indifferent. Even while talking to me they succeeded in
ignoring both my undressed condition and my own
embarrassment with such exquisite tact that I felt a surge of
warm gratitude toward them.

The old woman brought in a large tin basin and a tall
tin pitcher of lukewarm water. She handed me a sliver
of soap and a clean white towel, obviously purchased in
the United States and therefore in family use more than
ten years. I knelt on the floor by the basin and she poured

some water over my hands and then over my head. I soaped hands and face and she rinsed off the soap. I finished dressing. My friend's wife and I then had a glass of tea and I returned to my hotel. I was, thereafter, able to understand why, occasionally, my friend's wife would come to my hotel room and ask permission to take a bath in my bathroom. I thought it was a pretty shabby bathroom, but it did have hot water and a bathtub.

My second experience in a Russian home came only toward the end of my stay in Moscow. As incomes and relatively favored positions go in the Soviet Union, this family was by all standards very well off. The wife's salary was about five times the Russian average. The husband, a young and already distinguished scientist, was similarly well paid. But they lived in two and a half rooms, in a section of Moscow almost as remote as that in which my other friend lived, their apartment had no running water, and they used an outside privy. Sharing this space were the wife, the husband, his father, his mother, his grown sister, and two-and-a-half-year-old Sasha. Much of the husband's work was done at home, in one of the rooms which contained a three-quarter bed, a large desk above which was a shelf of books, and a wardrobe. There was space in it only for one chair in front of the desk. The main room was larger, and had a long dining table down the center and single cots arranged around its walls. There was another room which we did not see. And at one end of the large room only a curtain divided this family from another living in rooms beyond. Cooking was done on a little stove in the foyer.

Bearing in mind that these two families were in a far

better than average Soviet income bracket, and were in fact on the lower fringes of the Soviet elite, their circumstances will make it easier to visualize what is meant by one over-all Soviet statistic. The average Soviet citizen has dwelling space equal to six by nine feet of floor space, or little more than twice the size of an ordinary grave.

In 1934, an American visitor to Russia thoughtfully made notes on the prevailing retail prices of elemental necessities such as bread, potatoes and shoes and on his return to the United States carefully compiled a list of prices of the same items, as closely parallel in quality as could be found. His object was to find out what a Soviet rouble is really worth, and his researches proved it to have the buying power of two United States cents. In 1940, another American repeated the performance and came up with the same answer. In April, 1947, I did the same thing and found a rouble to be worth three cents. In December, 1948, a Norwegian trade delegation made a similar comparative shopping tour and found the rouble back again at two cents.

Between the time of my survey, and the one the Norwegians conducted, the Soviet currency had under-gone one of periodic shake-ups. New paper money was issued, and people possessing quantities of the old money were required to exchange it for the new at the ratio of ten old roubles for one new. This monetary stratagem meant that people who had been saving their money toward the purchase of a coat, a suit, or a pair of shoes had their savings, or power to purchase, reduced to one-tenth of what it had been with the old roubles.

Having thus safeguarded itself against a potentially disastrous run on its food and consumer goods stocks, the Soviet government abolished rationing, established a slightly revised scale of fixed prices without any appreciable revision of wage scales, and restored the rouble to its old, two-cent value.

By any standards it was a cruel trick to play on a people who had worked just as hard to earn the old roubles as they would have to work for the new. But it was not the first time the trick had been played, nor would it likely be the last. And it re-established, as an apparently fixed policy, the long-continued effort to keep the Soviet worker's rouble on a two-cent base. Keeping that value firmly in mind enables an American to gain a better understanding of what the Soviet living standard really is.

In dealing with the Soviet economy it is necessary always to remember that everyone works for the state. The state fixes wages, and it fixes the prices of goods the wages are to buy. Its over-all economic focus is not on the occasional worker who earns the big bonus, but on the mass of workers who earn the average. It is the mass who are most concerned and most affected by the manipulations by which the state, like the Lord, giveth and taketh away.

Any figure published by the Soviet government is subject to suspicion, since published statistics are more often used for propaganda than fact finding, but the government has said that it possesses a working force of 33,000,000 whose average wage is 450 roubles per month. This does not include the farm population of 88,000,000 or the millions who work for bare subsistence in slave-labor camps. But it does include all factory as well as office workers.

Among Soviet propagandists, and even official spokes-

man, there is always a certain amount of dispute about the
450-rouble average wage. Those who argue that it is too
low point out that nearly all manual and productive labor —
manufactures, mining, road building, etc. — is done on a
speed-up basis; incentive bonuses are paid for overfulfillment of norms. These incentive bonuses are sometimes
large and it is possible for a factory worker whose norm
pay is 900 roubles a month to earn, steadily, as much as
3,500 roubles monthly when his overfulfillment bonuses
are added to his base pay. Offsetting this argument is the
fact that most Soviet factory workers either from lack of
aptitude, indifference or malnutrition, do not qualify for
more than their norms and often do not even earn the norm,
and that bonuses are not paid the vast armies of clerical
workers and bureaucrats the 450 per month average
encompasses. Even if the 450 figure is low, the average is
very unlikely to exceed 550 to 600 roubles monthly.

Taking a family of four persons consisting of husband,
wife, and two children under fourteen and assuming that
both husband and wife work (as in most Soviet families
they do) and that each earns 550 roubles monthly, let us
see what happens to their monthly income of 1,100 roubles:

Rent	20
Electricity (enough for two 40-watt bulbs and one hot plate)	100
Heat (kerosene or wood)	60
Taxes (deducted at source)	110
Transportation	12
Share of House Fee to Janitor for cleaning communal toilet	10
Total, fixed charges	312

This leaves the family 788 roubles for all other expenses. Monthly costs for the plainest, most elemental foods run like this:

Bread (One pound per person per day) 275
Meat or fish (four pounds per person per month) . 272
Sugar (One and one-half pounds per person per
    month) 45
Butter (One and three-fifths pounds per person per
    month) 204
Cabbage (Two pounds per person per month) . . 144
Potatoes (Twenty pounds per person per month) . 76

It would not be difficult for this family to eat all this food every month. But since the cost of these quantities of these items is 1,016 roubles, and the family has only 788 to spend, they concentrate on bread and potatoes, the foods which provide bulk and are at the same time the cheapest. The average consumption of grain per person per year is 460 pounds, or one and one-third pound daily.

It is rare that this family can get through a month on a food expenditure of less than 500 to 600 roubles. More often it is more than 600. Taking 600 as an average, however, this leaves 188 roubles per month or 2,256 per year for all other purposes. Naturally they have to be clothed and these are samples of the prices they have to pay:

Man's suit   700 to 1,200 roubles
Woman's cotton dress   200 to 400
Child's dress   75 to 300
Adult's shoes   400 up
Child's shoes   200 up

One pair of shoes per year for each member of the family can account for more than half of everything left over after food and fixed charges. To say nothing of shirts, shifts, drawers, stockings, socks or the heavy, well-lined overcoats, galoshes and felt boots the winter climate demands. Usually the husband gets a new suit every three to four years, and the wife a new dress slightly oftener. Such figures make it easy to understand why Soviet citizens are so uniformly shabby. They also explain why Moscow needs only forty motion-picture theatres to serve a population of 7,000,000 persons and why, inside these theatres, the smell of uncleaned clothing is over-powering. Most people just don't have any money for movies or any clothes other than the ones they wear.

In the Soviet Union, the Communist propagandist shouts, medical care is free to everyone!

This statement, I found, is a compound half-truth. In the long run the citizen pays, with his labor, for everything the system does or provides. But medical service costs money in many other direct and indirect ways. More than that, an American reading such a statement is inclined to think the Soviet citizen gets for nothing the same *quality* of medical service that is available to the citizen of the United States, which is utterly false.

When a Soviet citizen becomes ill, he can go to a clinic for examination and treatment. Except in extraordinary instances, or when the sick person is of considerable importance doctors do not visit patients in their homes. If a sick person's wage is 350 roubles or less monthly, service is free and medicines are provided from the clinic dispensary. If it is more, a small fee is charged, and medicines must be bought and paid for at a pharmacy. If hospitalization is necessary there is always the problem of finding an empty bed, for the hospitals are always overcrowded, and in every Soviet hospital I visited, including Moscow's Kremlin Hospital which is reserved for very important people, beds occupied by seriously sick persons lined the corridors, leaving only narrow lanes through which visitors, doctors and nurses constantly passed. Anything approaching true asepsis is impossible and even elemental sanitation is rare.

The low fees which clinics and hospitals charge are only a part of the economic costs of sickness for the worker. Once, in Moscow, I came upon a set of facts concerning one worker which tell a great deal about the indirect costs.

The man involved in this case was a factory worker whose norm, or base pay, was 900 roubles a month. Over a long period of time, however, his speed-up bonuses had kept his pay level at 3,180 roubles per month. His direct taxes — an income tax, a tax on childlessness, an insurance tax and other items — amounted to about ten per cent of his pay and the government computed them on the basis of his total pay, thereby deducting 318 roubles monthly from his pay envelope. In addition, he was required to buy government bonds at the rate of ten per cent of his earnings, or another pay-roll deduction of 318 roubles. Thus 636 roubles were taken from his pay each month.

When this man became ill, with a heart attack which kept him in bed for a long period, his sick pay reverted to his norm pay of 900 roubles per month. But his tax and bond deductions were not revised, and so the factory deducted 636 roubles from his sick pay of 900 roubles, leaving him only 264 roubles per month on which to live. He survived only because his friends came to his rescue with loans they themselves could hardly afford. The government tax collectors and the factory management were utterly callous to his plight.

The economic costs of illness are, however, only a part of the problems of medical service. Another part is the quality of service that is dispensed. I had many contacts with Soviet medicine and my experiences were uniformly disillusioning. I can't say that I had expected it to be superlative, but I can say that I had not expected it to be so poor. One illustration is as good as any other.

In the belief that the educational value of a period of life in Russia would be worth while to him, I had my fourteen-year-old son join me there for a year. Several months before he was scheduled to return to the United States and school, he picked up an eye infection. We — my wife and I — took him to the principal eye clinic in Moscow, and with the aid of the Soviet Foreign Office, obtained the services of a doctor who was recommended as the best eye specialist in Moscow.

The clinic was an ancient building which seemed about to fall apart. Its wooden floors were bare and scuffed, its interior walls had not been painted in years and an occasional fly buzzed unheeded about the heads of long queues of people, some with infectious eye sores, waiting for the attention of a doctor. Being foreigners, we had the privileges of important people. We never had to wait.

The doctor was a tall, pleasant, courtly old gentleman of about seventy. He diagnosed the trouble as conjunctivitis. Thereafter, three times a week, my son went to the clinic where another doctor scraped the lids with a copper sulphate pencil. No anaesthesia of any sort was used. After each of these sessions he would come back to the apartment with his face distorted by pain. In addition to this treatment the doctor prescribed applications of a yellow, ophthalmic ointment. At the pharmacy where his prescription was filled, the pharmacist simply daubed a mound of the paste on a small sheet of cellophane-like paper, folded the paper over several times and handed it to us with a small glass rod one end of which was flattened like a spatula. The stuff was applied by scooping up a bit of the paste on the flat end of the rod and wiping it off against the under side of the lid. The little, long-nosed tubes in which such ointments are packed in the United States were unknown in Moscow.

After a month of this treatment, the eyes were no better. The specialist made another examination, and decided that it was not conjunctivitis but trachoma. Although it has been practically stamped out in most parts of the United States, trachoma is common in Russia. Eye specialists who deal with it often say it is easy to diagnose, and others who rarely see a case of it insist that it is difficult to recognize in the early stages. In any event our Moscow specialist had seen a lot of it in his time. After the second diagnosis he decided an operation would be necessary.

The anaesthesia used for the operation was novocaine, hypodermically injected into the eyelids. Then the lids were scraped with a scalpel. A bloody film covered the boy's eyes for four or five days afterward, virtually blinding him until it was absorbed. A month later, when we took him up to Sweden and put him on the *Drottningholm* for New York, his eyes were still inflamed. A New York specialist diagnosed the trouble as a type of conjunctivitis caused by a summer allergy, prescribed penicillin eye drops, and cleared it up in less than a week.

American specialists to whom I have told this story, when they get past the diagnostic performance, describe the Moscow specialist treatment as fundamentally sound, but archaic, more in conformity with practices of fifty years ago than those of today. This observation fits perfectly every bit of Soviet medicine I encountered, and from the Moscow specialist I learned at least one of the reasons why it remains on such a backward level. After the operation I asked the old doctor to let me do something for him. He replied: "The thing you can do for me is to get me subscriptions to the *American Journal of Ophthalmology* and the *Lancet* [a British medical journal]. I have not seen either of them in many years, and I would like to know what my colleagues in Britain and America are doing."

The proscription of foreign publications, even technical ones, is a police measure designed to safeguard the political ignorance of the Russian masses. But, as this instance shows, it directly affects their physical well-being.

Poor as it is, Soviet medicine stands up well in comparison with some other aspects of the "welfare" program such as, for example, the system of rest homes where workers, supposedly, take their vacations. In a little village near Moscow, where I rented a dacha one summer, I came to be pretty familiar with a typical rest home which was reserved for the use of members of a munitions workers union.

The place consisted of a number of smallish log huts, scattered through a grove of trees surrounding a pavilion-like big house where meals were served and gatherings held. The whole place was surrounded by a high log fence. Every morning on the stroke of six, a loud-speaker which, by actual test, was audible two miles away, sounded off with the voice of Radio Moscow, and continued until midnight with the mixture of news, sabre-rattling propaganda and music that Russian radios serve. Swimming was available in a muddy little river near by. Men and women who did not own bathing suits, and most did not, either waded in their underpants, or in nothing. Other recreation consisted of dancing in the evenings to a phonograph, or listening to lectures which parrotted the radio. Every two weeks the vacationers departed and a new batch of fifty took their places.

Funds for the maintenance of such places are provided by a pay-roll tax collected from Soviet enterprises, and administered by the central Council of Trades Unions. In fact, this appeared to be the principal function of the unions, since they have no real voice in the establishment of wage scales, and never call strikes.

From time to time, Kuznetsov, big boss of the trades unions, made reports which rang with boasts of how the Central Council had spent a billion roubles or more on rest homes. But analysis of the reports always revealed that expenditures amounted to no more than three or four roubles for each of the 33,000,000 members the unions claimed to have. The figure suggests the extent of the rest-home system. Five out of six Soviet workers never see one.

Another use for the welfare fund was indicated in a report of the Union of Railway Workers which announced that in 1945 it had spent 8 million roubles on the maintenance of clubs and "red corners" which are distribution points for Communist party propaganda. At such places workers whose roofs are leaking, whose shoes need mending and whose bellies are quite often empty are told that they are the most fortunate and well-tended workers in the world.

Soviet workers who survive to the age of sixty-five, and some do, are entitled to a pension. But these pensions run between 75 and 150 roubles per month, and figures already cited show how utterly impossible it is to sustain life on such a sum. Hence the Soviet citizen never stops working.

The government boasts that it has solved the problem of unemployment. In a sense, it has. But this does not mean, as it is often interpreted as meaning, that the slumps which produce unemployment in a free-enterprise system have been abolished. The Soviet Union has never had enough production to create an economic crisis, and at the rate it is going it is unlikely to have enough at any time in the foreseeable future.

One reason is that though everybody works at something, too few of them work at productive jobs. The economy operates against a self-perpetuating, and perpetually growing, drag of non-productive paper shufflers who write endless reports on the lack of production to other paper shufflers. They are simply people who put in a certain number of hours per day, six days per week, in order to get the pay envelope that will enable them to sustain a miserably housed, poorly clad, undernourished existence.

Millions of "employed" people are exemplified by the little man who, one day, walked into the wrong office, sat

down at a desk, and began rattling his papers. He did this
for three days before the office *nachalnik*, or chief, noticed
his alien presence. A checkup revealed that, in fact, he
belonged in the office of a totally different enterprise on
the floor below. Asked why he had not noticed he was in
the wrong place, he replied that he had paid some attention to the large number of new faces around him but, on
mature reflection, decided it would be best not to ask any
questions. Doubtless he was as useful in one office as the
other.

The Soviet solution of unemployment, in short, is
simply the creation of a permanent leaf-raking project. An
endless vista of hopeless poverty, garnished by a handful
of fifth-rate social services, is the security it provides for
the average individual.

Economic, or social, security has become the catch
phrase of the twentieth century. It means different things
to different people, and many things to many. We, in the
United States, define it as government protection against
joblessness; government aid in time of illness or disability;
pensions for the aged, the widowed, and the orphaned
group. Its ultimate meaning is: "Let the government take
care of me."

The Soviet government is one which has insisted on
assuming this responsibility in a total sense. What has happened there should be a lesson to all who yearn for it to
happen here.

Once, during my stay in Moscow, a Russian woman
showed me a letter she had received from a relative who
had emigrated to the United States many years before.
"By now," this Russian-American wrote, "I guess many of

us know that the workers' life in Russia is hard. But at least you do have security."

Despairingly, the woman who received this letter asked: "What security? Even if the police let us alone, the only security we have is to work until we die."

Since the beginning of the industrial revolution one of mankind's most persistent problems has been that of welding agriculture and industry into a harmoniously functioning economic whole. The farmer needs the produce of the factory as urgently as the factory worker needs the produce of the farm. A modern nation cannot be healthy with a sick agriculture any more than it can with a sick industry. Yet, however simple it may be to state the problem, solving it to the satisfaction of everyone involved is something that has not yet been accomplished anywhere. The Soviet Union is no exception.

As has been noted, Lenin's land program calling for the division of the land among landless peasants was designed more to capture their political support than to solve any economic problem. Since his grasp of economics was rudimentary at best, he probably had not foreseen that land reform would lower the total crop production. But when the great landed estates which had been farmed as business enterprises were broken up into plots of a few acres per peasant family, each family became interested primarily in feeding itself. They lacked draft animals and fertilizers, and, on their own, many proved far less efficient at making the land produce than when they had worked under skilled overseers. Thus the land, as a whole, produced less food and more of what was produced was con-

sumed on the land. Urban centers grew hungrier and
hungrier.

Lenin may have supposed that out of gratitude for the
land, the peasants would be happy to comply with government requisition of their crops. The Kronstadt uprising,
which was basically a peasant revolt, seems genuinely
to have surprised him. His inauguration of the New Economic Policy was, in effect, the gesture of Pilate — he
simply washed his hands of a seemingly insoluble problem by putting the peasants on a free-enterprise basis.

The result was inevitable. Some peasants, being more
highly skilled and better businessmen, became successful
while others sank lower into inept poverty. The kulaks, or
successful farmers, represented a new land-owning class
in its embryonic stages, a class whose economic interests
were antagonistic to any form of rigid state controls. By
1927 Stalin clearly understood this development for what
it was, a potential and potentially formidable challenge
to the Communist power.

But Stalin also recognized that for ten years Russian
industry had been at a virtual standstill. For three years
the ruling party, and to a lesser degree the nation itself,
had been rent by the battle for supremacy between Stalin
and Trotsky, from which Stalin emerged the victor and
Trotsky the banished. If he was to hang on to the power
he had gained, Stalin desperately needed some program
which would get the nation's industry going again, and
provide slogans to take the minds of the party and the
people away from the brutish slugfest that was going on
in the party's top levels. Seizing shamelessly upon ideas
which he had denounced two years before when they were

proposed by Trotsky, Stalin launched the first five-year plan.

Thus, in 1927, began the frenzied campaign to "overtake and surpass the capitalist states." At that time it was suggested that this might be accomplished in the first five years, but postponements became as regular a five-year event as the launching of new plans and at the end of four years of war the slogan was taken out of storage and shouted anew. Now, fulfillment is fixed for 1960, which is only a little more likely than 1932 was.

From the outset it was apparent that this frenzied concentration of man power and natural resources on an industrialization program could not be carried out with agriculture remaining unchanged. The fulfillment of the five-year plans demanded a massive transfer of farm populations to urban centers. It meant that the land would have to produce more, with less man power. The method Stalin chose to accomplish this was mechanization and collectivization. On paper, collectivized, mechanized farming makes economic sense. By any production standard it should be more productive. The difficulty, as Stalin found out, is that it runs counter to human nature. Every man who works the land wants to own the land he works, and Communist-style collectivization, whatever high-sounding phrases may be wrapped around it, is nothing more than a return to feudalism on a tractor.

The accomplishment of collectivization was entrusted directly to the Communist party, rather than any agency of the visible government. It required that the state take back from the peasants the land Lenin had urged them to seize. The peasants resisted fiercely and naturally the fiercest resistance came from the kulaks who had most to lose. Peasants buried their grain, slaughtered their cattle in the fields, and defiantly bared their breasts to the pistols of the Communist iron brooms. A good many thousands died that way, and literally hundreds of thousands more were carted off to Siberian slave camps.

Stalin won, of course, and the land was collectivized, but the first five-year plan ran its course in the midst of one of the most devastating man-made famines in history. In the end most of the human material left on the farms were those who had been the least spirited and the least efficient. The peasants who submitted were those who had the least to lose.

Now, there are two kinds of farms: the state farm, or *sovhoz*, and the collective farm, or *kolkhoz*.

The *sovhoz* usually consists of several thousand acres devoted to experimental planting and animal breeding where work is done by farm labor at fixed per diem wages.

The *kolkhoz* is the farm that produces for consumption. Its acreage may be anything from a few hundred to a few thousand. It spreads out around a village which is usually one wide, unpaved street, rutted and dusty in summer, miry in spring and fall, frozen in winter. Its houses are almost invariably pre-revolutionary and like those in Moscow and other cities, rotting from neglect. They are mostly one, sometimes two rooms, with thatched roofs. In parts of the Ukraine they are made of limestone which can be dug out of the ground, but elsewhere they are made of logs.

Each village has a clubhouse, where "agitators" come to make the political speeches which are the principal diversion offered the villagers, a nursery where field-working mammas can leave their young, a one-room school, and offices for the collective "chairman," as well as the "agronom," or agronomist, who is supposed to provide skilled advice and instruction and their clerical help. What used to be the village church usually serves as a granary, and there is sometimes a cooperative *magazin* or store which is most often locked because it practically never has anything to sell.

Each peasant family has its own cottage with a small back yard in which to tether a goat, keep a few chickens, or a pig or two. Seldom does any family have all these riches, and quite often it has none. In addition the family may have the personal use of a small strip, never more than an acre and usually some distance from the house, on which to grow its vegetables, potatoes, or whatever else is desired.

On the collectives males are always in short supply. The annual conscription takes away the boys as they turn nineteen, and many do not return. To a lesser, but still appreciable, degree the annual draft of fourteen-year-olds — both boys and girls — for the urban labor schools also serves as a constant instrument of village depopulation. Before the war, 55 per cent of Soviet agricultural labor was performed by women, and since then the figure has become much higher due to the enormous death toll the Red Army suffered.

A collective farm never possesses or controls its own tractors, reapers, binders, harrows, plows or other mechanical equipment. Mechanization is supplied through a system of Motor Tractor Stations, which are set up to serve not one, but several adjacent farms. The collectives have to pay, out of produce, for the services performed by the tractor stations. While this system provides for tighter control of the farms, which is what the Communist party wants, it also makes for waste. Plowing and harvesting quite often cannot be completed in all the areas a tractor station serves during the period when the weather is right, and the result is quite often loss of growing time or weather damage to crops, or both.

By design, Soviet tractors are larger and more cumbersome than the farms need. They are caterpillars which are intended to serve as farm implements, and also as prime movers for the Red Army. What this means is that the small tractors which an American farmer uses to perform many jobs such as sawing up his firewood are not available on the collectives and all such work must be performed by hand. The provision of mechanical power for such work by the tractor stations is regarded as unnecessary and wasteful. Water, even for the cattle barns, is mostly pumped by hand. The system of making tractors for peace or war has still another result. Manufacture is slower, initial cost is higher, and when war does come, the tractors are among the first casualties. The Soviet economy will be many years replacing the farm equipment it lost in the last war.

Since 1927, the word "plan" has become ubiquitous in the Soviet Union. A plan may be a blueprint for a factory, a budget for a university, a schedule of repair work to be done by a housing administration, or a demand for the production of so many tons of steel by a blast furnace. Agriculture is also planned. Each collective is given a specific directive detailing how many acres are to be planted in wheat, rye or vegetables, and how much of each, each farm is expected to produce. Only the weather cannot be planned, and in the planners' view it is often guilty of criminal sabotage.

In theory, whatever the collective farm produces is distributed like this:

Obligatory delivery to the state . . .	15 per cent
Payment to Machine Tractor Stations .	16
Service on sowing loan (for seed) . .	2
To reserves (for seed plus forage) . .	21.9
Social Fund (school, nursery, club, pensions etc.)	13.1
Sold to cooperatives or in free market .	5.1
Dividend in kind to workers	26.9

I repeat, in theory, this leaves for the collective farm workers slightly more than one-fourth of what the farm produces, to be distributed among themselves according to the amount of work each has contributed. But in fact the obligatory deliveries to the state are not fixed by percentage, but by arbitrary quotas which are changed from year to year. In bad years when production slumps, the quotas go up.

Delivery must be made to the state before any other charges are met. In any year that the total produce of the farm is not enough to meet the quota, the unfilled portion is carried over to the next year as a preferential charge. In terms of priority all the other state charges precede payments to the farm worker in the order named. Being the last to get paid, he sometimes does not get paid at all, because after all other charges are met there is nothing left.

This is the reason why, in years of severe drought, starvation begins at the very point the food is produced — on the collective farms. And even in the best years total payments to the collective workers never amount to 26 per cent of the farm's total produce. It is more often between ten and fifteen.

Collectivization's first fruit was catastrophe. Its second and more durable crop was peasant indifference. The human material on which the system was built was sullen, sluggish and passively hostile at the start. As time went on, and the promised better life did not materialize, it became utterly indifferent. The peasants gradually gave up all hope of self-betterment, and settled into a kind of despair. They will work no harder than they must to stay alive, and because of that their wage scales are deliberately rigged to make ever-present hunger their perpetual goad.

One of the functions of plan is to fix wage norms. Over the years, the state has steadily hiked the number of work days which it demands as a norm, from 200 to 230 to 248 until, in 1948, it was fixed at the impossible total of 260. Per year. A work day is not measured in hours of labor, but in quantity of tasks completed. To get credit for a work day a farm worker must plow so much land, or keep so many water troughs filled, and so on. Even the most energetic and willing farm workers find it impossible to turn in much more than 200 work days per year.

What the worker gets per work day depends on how well the collective meets its quotas. The productive worker's share, however, is partly drained off by non-producers who are, nevertheless, a part of the collective's pay roll. The chairman, who is in theory elected by the collective workers and in fact appointed by the Communist party, must have a staff of timekeepers, bookkeepers and other administrative assistants. The *agronom*, or technician, similarly needs clerical help to keep the crop records. There are storekeepers, granary watchmen, day and night guards to prevent pilferage of the vegetable fields, a teacher for the school and nurses for the nursery. The workers do not simply go into the fields and work, they must go in brigades or squads with a brigadier or squad leader in charge of each. He, or she, also is a drone. All of these people are, like the worker, paid out of what the collective produces. In a good year, on a fertile farm, the worker's 200 work days may return him: 600 roubles in cash, 880 pounds of grain, 1,000 pounds of potatoes, 1,000 pounds of vegetables and 800 pounds of hay.

The operations of the army and labor conscription systems have produced an unusual population situation on collectives. On an average, every adult has one, and quite often two, non-working dependents, consisting of aged parents or small children. With his wage in kind, the worker must feed not only himself, but others. Most keep the grain for their own food, the hay for their animals, and try to sell or barter their potatoes and vegetables for meat and/or clothing. Getting a new pair of shoes is a far more complex operation for the collective worker than for the factory worker — difficult as that has been shown to be. In the course of a lifetime the peasant sees far less of the produce of factories than factory workers see of his. In fact, it is the peasant who is the main prop of the Soviet economy, and next after slave labor its most shabbily fed, clothed and housed element.

It is the peasant's effort to convert his potatoes and vegetables into roubles for meat, shoes and pants that helps create one strange and persistent feature of Soviet city life. This is the "free market," which is found in all Soviet cities, large and small. Usually it is simply a city square to which both urban and rural dwellers come with things to sell — items that range from rusty nails and chromos of the Blessed Virgin to homemade brassières and hair nets to meat and potatoes. Soviet leaders look with disfavor on these markets because, in a planned economy, they are an anomaly. If the planners' plans really worked, they would be unnecessary.

But the failure of the distributive system to distribute properly, contributes as much to their continued existence as does the necessity of the peasant to sell his food for clothing. Very often when the urban householder goes to the stores to buy potatoes, vegetables or other items, the store has none. Either his inadequate allotment has been sold, or his supplier has failed to make deliveries, or in some other way the pipe line has been clogged by bureaucratic indifference, red tape, or knavery. In any event, the failure of the regular channels of supply force the urban householder to go to the market where, usually, the price is higher than the controlled price. To the worker's family this will mean even less money for clothing, to the peasant it may mean the difference between a winter in straw shoes and one in felt boots.

But distribution of farm products to the cities, however spotty and inefficient, is infinitely superior to distribution of manufactured goods to the farm villages. In fact, it can be said that the latter simply does not exist.

The Soviet planners have left this phase of the operative economy in the hands of cooperatives which are, in essence, combined manufacturing and mercantile barter enterprises. In its table of distribution, the collective is allowed to sell five per cent of its produce to the cooperatives which is supposed to pay with shoes, stockings, utensils, household goods, etc., made in cooperative factories for distribution to the collectives.

In order to encourage this kind of exchange, cooperatives have been given many special privileges such as tax reductions, enlarged profit margins, long-term loans from government funds, and so forth. But, in 1947, for example, the production quota for the factories involved in the entire cooperative movement came to startlingly low totals. For the whole year, the cooperatives promised to produce 375 million buttons, 23 million pairs of stockings, and 500 thousand beds. For the 88 millions who live in collectives, this meant four and a quarter buttons each; one stocking per woman, one bed for forty families. Even if the chairmen, agronoms and brigadiers on the collectives stopped snaring everything for themselves and made an honestly equable distribution, which seems unlikely, it would still take forty years to provide a new bed for each collective farm family.

When they feel safe from the police, the peasants sometimes sing the following bootleg song:

> If there were no winter,
> There would be no freezing.
> If there were no Soviets,
> Hunger'd not be teasing.

In the cemetery,
Red the poppy borders,
Stalin leads us all there
Says it's Lenin's orders.

Kolkhoz, kolkhoz, kolkhoz,
You are all our woe —
You have brought starvation,
Caused our tears to flow.

Never do we dance now,
Never see much gladness,
Five-year-plan production
Drives us all to madness.

No matter what *Pravda* and the propagandists say, after thirty years of Communist rule the major preoccupation of the Russian people is not culture, not politics, not education or even war and peace, but the elemental trinity of life — food, clothing and shelter.

Of these, the chiefest is food, as the following indignant item from the newspaper *Vechernaya Moskva* (Evening Moscow) illustrates:

Once upon a time there was a district militia chief. [*Militsia* is the Russian word for ordinary police.] It occurred to this chief that he would like some cream, so he bought a cow. Then he wanted goat's milk, so he bought two goats. Then he hungered for ham, so he bought two pigs. In the district militia station people whispered: "Where do you think he will put the livestock department?" But the chief did not wonder — he acted. In no time at all a big shed materialized in his yard and into it went the cow, the goats and pigs. Then was heard more nervous whispering: "How is he going to feed them?" But fodder was found. The chief requisitioned it from the nearest collective farm free of charge. Rumors spread that the chief of the district militia was also a magician.

But judge for yourself. Last winter the employees of his station provided for their own needs, with their own hands, twelve cubic meters of firewood. The chief ordered them to stock it in the yard of his house where it would be under his eyes. The wood disappeared. It was found on the public market where the chief's wife had sold it. But this was not the only thing sold on the market. Sometimes the chief would say to a militiaman on duty: "I have killed a pig. We cannot eat everything, there is meat and fat left over. Go to my home and get about sixty pounds and sell it on the market." So a militiaman sold pork on the market. No one could interfere since pork trade was authorized by the chief of the district militia.

Now this is no fable. This district chief is no fairy tale personage but lives in Moscow. He is in charge of the 67th district and his name is I. I. Zatzarinsky. Not only is he real, his cows and pigs and goats are also real and the ten thousand rubles he paid for the cow was real money. Only its origin was obscure.

But to inhabitants of the 67th district the work of the district chief is not real. In their territory there are frequent cases of robbery and misbehavior. Recently the chief-magician performed a new feat of magic — all militiamen vanished from their district posts. On order of the chief they had all gone to the collective farm village of Schnitnikovo in another region to stand guard over the crops of the collective farm. For this the collective farm gave Zatzarinsky five tons of potatoes. He kept one, gave two to the militia chief of that region and two were divided among the militiamen who did guard duty.

A simple Soviet citizen who goes to the 67th district station for help can always expect the standard answer: "The chief is busy." But if he has deals to make the chief is never busy.

Except in the most corrupt communities, any such story about a police chief in any American community would lead to such a furore as to make a ninety-day scandal. But in Moscow, this little piece dropped without reported aftermath, and as far as the papers ever revealed that chief is still in his job and still ignoring robbers in favor of livestock, firewood and farm produce.

What's wrong with the Soviet economy? Why has it fallen so miserably short of the utopia its theories promised it would provide?

Facing this question, some people who are familiar with the real situation tend to lay much blame on the over-balanced emphasis Soviet planners have placed on the development of heavy industry. They say, accurately enough, that since 1927 and for many years to come the nation's heavy-industry production has been and will continue to be plowed back into still more heavy industry. They point out that at present and for a long time to come the products of existing steel mills are being and will be used first to build more steel mills, and after that to construct rail transport, agricultural machinery, mining equipment and motor trucks with priorities in the order named. To this factor they add the unknown X of armament. None but the Kremlin hierarchy knows how much Soviet steel was used in 1949 to make guns, tanks, airplanes, prime movers and hobnails for Red Army boots, but by all the signs the quantity was a large part of total Soviet production. From this it is argued that the Soviet citizens are poor because there is too little left over for factory tools to make shoes, textiles, furniture or nails for workers' housing.

I do not and cannot disagree with all this, but I do not

think it goes deeply enough. It implies an eventual attainment of Soviet goals without any alteration of present methods, which I do not regard as likely. After living in Moscow, studying its press, watching the operations of its economy and the people who live by, with and under it, I concluded that the real explanation of the system's conspicuous lack of success is the system itself.

In the first instance, the system is responsible for the abysmal inefficiency of its factories, mines, farms and other productive enterprises.

Totally planned economy means total state responsibility for every phase of activity carried on within the state, and state responsibility requires state control. In the Soviet Union control manifests itself in two forms of supervision, political and administrative.

To meet the demands of the system, a Soviet factory requires not one, but two or three directors. There is a production director whose training is that of an engineer and whose responsibility is to make the factory go. If he happens to be a Communist party member, as he sometimes is, he may also be the factory's personnel boss, but if he is not, then the factory must have a director of cadres whose job it is to represent the party in the selection and promotion of factory personnel. When the production director wants to make a foreman out of a man who is competent, and conscientious, but not a party man, and the director of cadres wants to promote a less competent party member, it is the party member who gets the job. Efficient operation is thereby reduced that much.

At the production director's other elbow is an MVD officer whose powers are ubiquitous. His assignment is to keep an eye out for enemies of the state. Any factory employee can become an enemy of the state if he makes a mistake the MVD man decides is due to a "politically negative" attitude. The MVD man has complete access to all records, can question any employee at any time, and constantly connives to make one employee spy and report on the other. His capacity to disrupt factory rhythm merely by the exercise of suspicion is unbelievable. One hour in his office will destroy a worker's ability to concentrate for days. The production director who is least immune of all the factory personnel lives and works in the knowledge that any show of independence on his part might be interpreted by the MVD man as evidence of intent to commit dangerous sabotage. For self-protection he clears every problem and decision, including emergency ones, with his ministerial higher-ups in Moscow. Consequent loss of factory time, which means production, is enormous.

Administrative control is a loss of another color. It creates an additional burden on production by saddling every productive enterprise with costly quantities of non-producing employees. One factory director gives this picture: "As a rule, there are thirty audits a year. Each auditor does his job down to the last rouble, but, since they are not required to show whether the factory operated at a profit, they do not do so. As a result of this system, factory directors are often reproached for minor violations of rules, but nobody is interested in whether, on the whole, he does a good or a bad job of running the factory. A factory has to draw up enormous heaps of forms, which often duplicate one another, and send five or six copies to one and the same office. Each month our factory prepares more than 50 accounting forms. This abundance of accounting is partially explained by the fact that the director has everything planned for him, and has to give an account of every single thing."

Paper work, I might add, is mostly done by hand. Soviet office equipment rarely consists of anything more time-saving than a typewriter and an abacus.

A fair indication of the extent to which Soviet production is burdened in this way, as compared to American production, was provided during 1945 by the high-brow Soviet magazine *Problems of Economy*. It contrasted a Urals coal mine with one near Pittsburgh, and showed that the Urals mine turned out one-third the volume of coal the Pittsburgh mine produced but kept an office staff of 67 persons, compared to eight in the American mine's office. Then it set an electric power station at Kemerovo against one at South Amboy, New Jersey. The two plants produced the same volume of electricity; the Soviet one maintained a pay roll of 480 persons with 91 doing office work, against a pay roll of 51 persons with 17 in the office at the American plant.

In 1948, the *New York Times* printed a short article which indicated how easily and imperceptibly such lavish use of non-productive personnel can mount into the millions. It reported a decree which ordered the collective farms to transfer 500,000 of their office workers out into the fields. Half a million persons peremptorily shifted from desk to plow! It sounds stupendous — but it meant the transfer of only two persons per farm. And the farms already averaged 130 field workers each.

"Well," I have heard people say, "if the government runs everything, what does it matter? It just means taking the money out of one pocket and putting it into the other."

True enough. But it also means that as long as the system stays the way it is, every expansion of productive capacity will carry with it an expansion of the non-productive personnel the system requires, and thus, no matter how many new factories are built, prices will have to stay high, as they now are, and wages low, as they now are. The only real change possible is a change in the system itself, and as long as the Communists who built the system continue to be its principal beneficiaries, change is unlikely.

The fantastically high costs of production, however, are only part of the explanation for the general level of poverty. It does not explain, for instance, why the potatoes, which the government most surely collects at the farm, are so often missing from the city stores to which they are supposed to go.

Evidence of this kind of maldistribution is to be encountered on every hand. Once, on a routine civilian flight from Moscow to Odessa, the airplane I was in put down at Kiev, a city of more than half a million persons. We had to spend a night there because, as the airport *nachalnik* explained, there was no gasoline to refuel the plane at Kiev. At first I was startled. Was Russia as short of gasoline as that? I asked myself. But there had been gasoline in Moscow when we left, and there was gasoline in Odessa when we eventually arrived. So, obviously, Kiev had been temporarily out of gasoline only because somebody, somewhere, for some reason or none, had failed to deliver it.

Again, in Odessa, the Hotel London in which I was

staying ran out of food, or at least the manager said it had. But without difficulty I went to the free market and bought tomatoes, lettuce, onions, eggs, and a number of other food items which I took back to the hotel and had prepared. I could also have purchased meat and milk, but prudently refrained from doing so because the meat was a little too flyblown and I never drink milk anywhere outside the United States. So, obviously, there was no real shortage of food, and the failure of the hotel supply was either a stoppage in the particular pipe line which served the hotel, or a stratagem on the part of the manager to make a few roubles for himself, since he charged me the full price for the meals his kitchen prepared from the food I brought in.

On another occasion I sent a telegram from Odessa to my office in Moscow. It was written in Russian so as to cause no translation difficulties and MVD suspicions in the telegraph office, and I paid an exorbitant premium for "lightning" service to ensure prompt delivery. I got back to Moscow eight days later, and the telegram was delivered the day after I arrived.

From these and other experiences it was apparent that distribution suffered greatly at the hands of the bureaucracy. All distribution is, like the postal and telegraph systems, essentially a service industry. In a free enterprise, the person or firm who gives the best service is the one who usually gets the business. When the profit incentive is removed, speed and reliability are lost.

Yet, there was another aspect which I came to believe had a very great bearing on the general lack of efficient distribution. A startling number of people seemed to be engaged in the diversion of goods from regular channels, either for their own use or for illegal sale. I have noted the behavior of the Politburo member Scherbakov who had his easy chairs made in a factory which should have been producing for the front, as well as the housing repair man who diverted his official funds to pockets unascertained and the police chief who bartered the services of his subordinates for potatoes.

This sort of thing, I gradually learned, has become a national disease. Once, in Moscow, I needed to purchase 1,000 large envelopes for the filing system maintained in my office. At the regular commercial store the envelopes I wanted were eight roubles each; the number I needed would have cost more than $600 at the exchange rate the government fixed for my dollars. I tried to get them through an agency called Burobin, a mercantile bureau for foreigners maintained by the Ministry of Foreign Affairs. They said they had none, and could not get any. I was about to give up when a Russian friend stepped into the picture. He said he knew a factory director who made the kind of envelopes I wanted. Next day he brought me a proposition. The director would let him have the envelopes for 300 roubles ($25 compared to the commercial price of more than $600) provided I would lend him my automobile for a day. This kind of a deal was strictly illegal, and it meant that somewhere 1,000 envelopes would disappear from distributive channels the planners had planned them for. But I wanted the envelopes and the director got the car for a day, which he probably used to get involved in some other, equally unsocialistic barter.

A more revealing sample is the story of a friend who

acquired a house on the outskirts of town. The place needed repairs and painting, and Burobin provided the workmen and the materials for a flat fee to be paid Burobin. For three weeks the workmen dawdled over a job that should have taken three days at most. During this time my friend decided he would like to have a dilapidated porch on the house refloored, and walled in with glass and wood for an extra bed-sitting room. He mentioned the matter to Burobin and was told the materials were not available. He mentioned it to one of the workmen and was told that, for 3,000 roubles, the workmen would get the materials and do the work, but only on condition that the matter must never be mentioned to Burobin. My friend handed over the roubles. Next day the men turned up with all the necessary materials in a truck and, after spending three weeks to get a three-day job done, did a good week's work in three days. And did it well.

The Russian people have developed a post-revolutionary word for such deals; they are called *blat*. The word has its origin in old prison slang. *Blatnoi* was originally used to designate a prisoner who fawned upon his warden in order to obtain a favor or privilege. Russians nowadays define *blat* as "working the left." It means any kind of deal which, though forbidden by law, is generally acceptable to society akin to the manner in which Americans entertained bootleggers during the prohibition era. They go further, and say that it is *blat* that keeps the country going.* If that is so, and it well might be, it means that the land of Communist party socialism has been taped at the seams with under-the-counter free enterprise.

* The phrase occurs in Godfrey Blunden's novel, *Room on the Route* (J. B. Lippincott Co., 1947), but it was not original with him.

Chapter VIII

‖‖

THE EMANCIPATION OF WOMEN

‖‖

NOT long ago two men I know met for the first time. One was a diplomat on vacation from his Moscow station, the other a correspondent who had not visited the Soviet Union in ten years. "So you've been in Russia?" the correspondent asked. "Tell me, are the women still doing all the work there?"

This opener provoked a serious two-hour conversation, because it was a good deal more than the wisecrack it could be mistaken for. In fact, it was a sharp appraisal of the place of women in the Soviet scheme.

Except for the highest levels of Communist party leadership, such as the Central Committee or the Politburo, there is no job category that does not contain women. There are women judges and lawyers, scientists, physicians, factory directors, engineers, technicians, sub-executives and clerks. There are also women truck drivers, crane operators, locomotive drivers and firemen, printers, stevedores, roustabouts, sandhogs, subway guards, and street cleaners. Between men and women, equality of economic opportunity is nearly absolute.

Soviet women at work are always impressive. On a job of manual labor the average Soviet male acts as if he is bored stiff or too tired to falter another step, or both. At the same tasks women are almost uniformly energetic. I had vaguely noticed this several times around Moscow

when watching mixed construction gangs at work. But it
hit me hardest in the Donbas town of Voroshilovgrad
where, on the balcony of a little hostel, I spent half an
hour sidewalk-superintending a platoon of men and
women as they cleared up bomb rubble in a yard across
the street. The women worked vigorously and steadily
while the men, after every few minutes of back bending
and stone pitching, retired to the shade to loll on the stones
for a smoke and a gossip.

Always anxious to put the most misleading thought forward, my Foreign Office conducting officer explained that
after the long war the men were tired. When I checked
this with an old-timer, he snorted: "Hmpf — no lazier now
than before the war." Further ferreting produced a rational
explanation. Under the speed-up system, the more the
gangs accomplish, the more money they receive. This was
a sufficient incentive to make the women, and particularly
those with children, work extra hard in order to offset the
laziness of their male comrades and to hoist the whole
group to a higher pay bracket. When the men discovered
this feminine willingness they promptly took advantage
of it, as men have always done and always will.

If we discount the extra burden this deplorable male
attitude throws on Soviet women, then it is perfectly true
they have two things women elsewhere think are desirable — equality of opportunity and equality of pay. In
the Communist party state, however, work is not a woman's
choice but a duty and necessity. The state lives by the
rule that each citizen shall contribute according to his
ability, and be paid according to what he contributes —
and Soviet women are also Soviet citizens. While it is

doubtful if many could be induced to take jobs by anything as abstract as a duty laid down in a constitution, a state which controls everything finds it no problem to make wages and prices serve as an enforcement agency. By keeping wages below what a man needs to feed and clothe a family in which the wife is not a wage earner, it is easy to make women work, whether they want to or not. Now, in addition, the Soviet government has applied the speed-up to the production of children.

In its thirty years of existence, the attitude of the state towards women as mothers has undergone profound changes. When the revolution was young, Alexandra Kollontai, the beautiful advocate of free love and female emancipation, rallied Russian womanhood with the cry: "Cast off your chains! Do not be slaves to religion, to marriage, to children." On this platform, she got abortion legalized, made marriage and divorce as easy as an illiterate's X mark in a bureaucrat's ledger, and provided a rudimentary sort of state care for expectant mothers, orphans and illegitimate children. Never in the history of any state had women come closer to total sex freedom. Ever since, the pendulum has been swinging back, closer and closer to total sex serfdom.

The first big swing was in 1936 when abortion was outlawed and a system of bonuses for babies substituted. Eight years later this was followed by a still more drastic decree. Soviet propagandists and apologists have deliberately covered up or ignored some of the provisions of this act, which is now law, because it is not a pretty thing and certainly would not win friends for Communism. But it defines the position of women in the Soviet Union today more clearly than the Soviet constitution or any other state document.

The decree's first provision sets up a new system of baby bonuses under which lump-sum payments begin with the third child, instead of the seventh as previously provided, and offers monthly subsidies until the child reaches the age of five plus an ascending scale of cash prizes. As supplemental inducements, it halves the nursery and kindergarten fees for low-income mothers of three or more children, increases maternity leaves from 63 to 77 days, and provides medals such as the Order of Maternal Glory and the Order of Mother Heroine for mothers of nine or ten children.

The Motherhood medals are not always the prideful badges they were intended to be. In a village not far from Moscow there lives a little old woman who reared ten children. When the law was announced, she proudly went in to ask for her Mother Heroine's medal. But when the authorities checked her list of offspring, they found that one of her daughters had married an American and had fled to live among the wicked capitalists of the United States. "That child," they sternly told her, "never existed." Instead of Mother Heroine, they bonged her with Maternal Glory for nine children — but the old woman seldom wears her medal. It saddens her to think that the one child who remembers her with parcels of food and clothing, is a child that never was.

The new law also attempts to stimulate the production of children by unmarried women, offering them monthly payments of 100 roubles for one child, 150 for two and 200 for three. At the same time it releases men from any legal inhibitions they may previously have suffered by abolishing male responsibility for illegitimates. The law now reads: "The right of a mother to appeal to a court with a request that the court establish paternity and order the payment of alimony for the maintenance of a child of which the father is a man with whom she has not contracted a registered marriage is revoked."

Next the decree cracks the whip on bachelors and career gals. Regardless of whether married or not, women between the ages of 20 and 45, and men 20 to 50, are required to pay a tax for childlessness. Those with no children must pay six per cent of their earnings, one child, one per cent; two children calls for one half of one per cent. Adopted children count as much as natural ones.

Kollontai's pen-scratch divorces were also abolished. The law took divorces out of the hands of the Registry Offices, called ZAGS, and put the courts in charge. It is now necessary for a person seeking a divorce to make formal court application, advertise his or her intentions in a local newspaper, produce the other contracting party in court, agree to follow court instructions for attempted reconciliations and finally submit to court orders for the division of property (which rarely consists of anything more than clothing and household effects) and the custody of children.

These are formidable barriers. Court calendars are crowded and it usually takes the newspapers months to find space for the ads. But the decree has a final economic twist which, for the mass of citizens, is the biggest hurdle of all. On filing a divorce application the applicant must pay a court fee of 100 roubles, and on the issuance of a certificate one or both parties must pay not less than 500 and up to 2,000 roubles. The formerly free-and-easy divorce is now too costly for the average citizen.

Divorces are, however, still being had and sometimes the court fees are not the only ones involved. Nowadays, when one marriage partner wants to get clear as speedily as possible, it is often necessary to bribe the other to cooperate. One such case involved a pretty dancer who fell in love with, and eventually married, a minor functionary in one of Moscow's foreign embassies. When she told her Soviet husband of her desire for a divorce he threatened every obstruction he could think of until her fiancé bought him off with a suit of clothes, a typewriter, a camera, a carton of American cigarettes and half a dozen cans of corned beef hash. By Soviet standards the lady came high.

The last paragraph of the new law on motherhood, bastardy, tax-punished barrenness and divorce makes it apparent that the lawmakers in the Kremlin are ashamed of it. The paragraph reads: "The Public Prosecutor's organizations, in accord with legislation now in force, shall prefer criminal charges against anyone . . . who offends or lowers the dignity of motherhood." What this means is that Mom and Stalin are now in the same bracket. A ribald joke known to everyone in Russia, but much too broad to print, can fetch its teller ten years in a Siberian slave-labor stockade.

The baby bonuses are not big enough to permit women to give up their jobs. They simply make childbearing a source of pin money. In the villages this may produce more babies, but in the cities more children will be born, or adopted, to escape the tax on childlessness than to collect any bonus. For the urban woman, life is already too rigorous to take on the added chores of a big family.

Propagandists seldom say the same things other people do. Knowing that women would receive this new law with grumbling anger, the Kremlin ordered the Soviet press to try to kid them into thinking the government really was interested in improving their welfare. It is doubtful whether the campaign that followed accomplished its purpose, but it did provide a spate of items which told a lot about how Russian women live.

As before the decree, marriage remains easy. All any couple has to do is go to a Registry Office and sign up. Following this tack, one phase of the crusade was an attempt to make the Registry Offices more attractive to young brides. This is how *Moskovsky Bolshevik* went about it:

> The theme is the old, but eternally new theme of love uniting two young hearts. They are happy. They go to ZAGS accompanied by friends and relations. The writers of romances at this point usually write a happy and quite understandable full stop.
>
> At the Egorevsk ZAGS, however, the affair is not concluded so well. It is a gray, gloomy building. As the young people step over the threshold the bride says in a frightened tone, "It is so dark, I can see nothing." The bridegroom produces a flashlight from his pocket and throws a dim ray upon a dingy room with torn wallpaper, a cobweb hanging from the ceiling, and a decrepit bench along the wall upon which an aged woman is weeping. One of the party asks if they have come to the right place, but unfortunately there is no mistake.
>
> They go through into a second room, just as cold and un-

welcoming. There is a wooden table covered with a soiled ink-stained cloth. Behind the table sits the registrar in her overcoat, felt boots and scarf. She raises her expressionless eyes towards the party and says in a dreary voice: "Next! Who has died?"

The young people are surprised and uncomfortable. When the groom explains they have come to get married, and not to register a death, they are told to go outside and wait and the tearful old woman is called in. The young couple and their guests return to the outer room; someone tries to jest but no one laughs. Through the half-opened door is heard the voice of the tearful old woman bewailing the loss of her husband.

Finally the young people are summoned. The climax of the whole affair is reached when the time comes to sign the document and it is discovered that the ink is frozen in the inkpot. They have to warm it by the most simple means — human breath.

This is no invention but the truth. . . . One would like to ask those in charge of the Registry Offices if they ever had a happy wedding day.

If love overcomes the gloom of the ZAGS offices, the morning after also has its hazards, and the Novosikbirsk radio told of some of them in a skit called "Why They Parted." It showed a couple getting acquainted with the stuff they had bought to set up housekeeping. Handles came off the cups, can openers distintegrated against the jam jar, and the bride's make-up mirror was so poor she got her lipstick on her ear. Their tempers cracked, they quarreled and the bride walked out.

Still, the papers assumed that marriages would survive such crises, for they went on to complain of other things, one of which concerned layettes. Pointing out that in its solicitude for mothers the benevolent state had arranged to provide them with "state layettes," the press found that in many places the bureaucrats were falling down on distribution, and upbraided them mercilessly. Naïvely I assumed that the object of so much to-do, the layette itself must be something special. It proved to consist of a thermometer, two rubber nipples, a square yard of muslin, a square yard of rubber sheeting, a can of boric-acid powder and a small tube of vaseline. To get this much from an ever-thoughtful state the Soviet mother was required to hand over 30 roubles, equivalent to two days' pay at the average wage. The American mother can buy the same items of better quality for three hours' work at the American wage level.

Then the papers turned their guns on another supply problem. *Izvestiya*, the government newspaper, attacked the authorities of the city of Kalinin (pop. 216,000) for having only "one shop to supply supplementary rations to expectant and nursing mothers, some of whom have to walk as much as five or six kilometers." *Izvestiya* continued:"The rations are irregularly supplied and one has to be on the spot when they come in order to get one's share. There is only one milk supply shop which is located on the far side of the Volga and queues begin to form early in the morning although milk is not delivered until two or three in the afternoon. The head of the trading department recently descended on the shop and forbade the sale of more than one-half litre [about one pint] at a time to any one person. This means that from now on women will have to lose 24 days a month to get their milk." Since no Soviet

worker can stay off the job 24 days a month and keep out
of jail, what it really meant was that many babies would
have to get along without any milk at all.

Soviet newspapers do not print such stories except when
they are attacking a general situation. One Soviet woman
remarked: "There was no need to go to Kalinin for that
item. They could have found dozens of examples right
here in Moscow."

However dismal, this picture is far from complete. For
external consumption, Soviet propagandists talk about
the state-supported nurseries where working women leave
their children and go blithely on to toil. It's a pretty design
for working motherhood — with two important facts missing. First, nurseries and kindergartens have to be paid as
in any capitalist state, and many women can't afford them.
Second, there are not, and never have been, enough nurseries to take care of all the children.

Since women cannot hold a job and tend a baby at the
same time, even one child can be a big problem. Some
women solve it by having their mother, mother-in-law, or
an elderly unattached woman live with them. This often
creates additional emotional strain because it further
plugs up housing which is already abysmally overcrowded.

Most Soviet families cook in a communal kitchen shared
by two to six families. I have read articles which extolled
these kitchens as one of the bright facets of Soviet life,
describing them as an ecstatic haven where a blissful sis-
terhood swaps inspiration to carry on the great tasks of
Building a New Society. Nothing could be sillier. First try
to picture three or four women with nerves already frayed
by a long day's work, at least one sick baby, and the frus-

trations of trying to find food in half-empty shops. Then put them together on one stove, one sink, one faucet and one small table, all hurriedly trying to get their own dinner together. Quite often it results in pulled hair, blacked eyes, caustic soda in a neighbor's soup, or vituperative brawling that brings the cops on the double.

The kitchens are not the only places where raw nerves result in flying fists. Women also brawl in public places. One instance involved a Red Army female surgeon identified as Comrade L. and a streetcar conductress named Demkina. Comrade L. broke the law by getting on a streetcar at the front end. Conductress Demkina ordered her to get off and to enter at the rear. The lady surgeon demurred and Demkina popped her, first on the chest where hung her seven military decorations — and then on the nose. The fracas that ensued put Comrade L. in the nearest hospital.

It was not accidental that Demkina's first punch was aimed at the medals. Those jingling bangles were a symbol — they betokened the fact that Comrade L.'s station in life was on a level higher than that of a tramway conductress. With many Soviet women the dissatisfactions of a hard life have been turned to bitterness by the rise of a whole group of privileged classes. The wife of a commissar or general can have servants, fine furs, silken underwear, dyed hair, imported perfume and get ostentatiously fat. Among her less-favored sisters, however, nothing inspires as much envy or despair as the manner in which these upper-bracket women are able to dress their children.

The late Mikhail Kalinin, who sometimes played the

part of a sort of Bolshevist Mr. Alexander, once received a letter from a working mother. She related that her little daughter sat at the same desk in school with the daughter of a highly paid actress. The child had become envious of the pretty dresses and good shoes her companion wore and had demanded an identical ensemble. By working additional hours at the factory her mother managed to buy it, but when the child wore her new outfit to school, the actress' daughter turned up in a still newer and more glamorous *décor*. "What shall I do?" the working mother asked. "I cannot fulfill the wishes of my daughter and she is nagging me." Kalinin's answer was a severe reprimand. "You have failed," he chided, "to bring up your daughter as a modest and thrifty girl with respect for the work of her parents."

Traditionally Russian women were renowned for their warmth and femininity. Today that tradition largely survives in the professional or intellectual class, a minority which is sandwiched between the fat wives of the upper crust and the ready-fisted toiling mass. Its relative size is indicated by the fact that two to three million little girls enter Soviet kindergartens each year, of which one in forty reach the universities. But it is an important force, because it is composed of actresses, ballerinas, lawyers, scientists, engineers and other specialized trades. Nowhere else in the new class structure is the conflict between the hardships of life and the normal sex instincts of warm-blooded women raising such psychological hob.

These are the women who are usually the most attractive. They know how to dress with taste, conduct themselves with restraint, and create the sort of home in which a child can grow up in the atmosphere which makes the best citizens everywhere. For all its advantages, however, this is the most nearly childless segment in the Soviet Union, perhaps because it is the best educated and most sensitive. A large percentage of the women in this group have no offspring at all; most of the rest have one child or a maximum of two. In a land where abortion is outlawed and birth-control devices virtually unknown, this takes a bit of doing. These women live in fear of pregnancy, which tends to make them shrewish. Beneath their soft curves and pretty faces they carry a core of steel — much too hard ever to be bent by baby bonuses or similar state inducements.

For them, the key is Kalinin's "respect for work," a maxim for all Soviet women except the new-rich wives of the commissars. They know that what happened to Sofia Zabotkina, a rebel, could happen to any of them. Sofia was so fed up with her job that one day she played hookey. For that she was hailed into a court and sentenced to four months' forced labor, which means she was fined one-fourth of her pay for one-third of a year, which she was required to work out on the job. Her boredom changed to open rebellion. For ten more days she stayed home, then the cops came again. Now Sofia is doing five years in a Siberian "correctional labor" camp. She lives behind barbed wire and is a slave in an institution where another such display could mean her sudden end.

Emotional lethargy is endemic among Soviet women, and it is not easy to throw off. Once, in Moscow, a friend noticed that his Russian secretary, a normally cheery girl, had been drooping for several days. After worrying for a while, he came out with a direct question, "Are you in any kind of trouble?"

"*Nyet,*" she said tiredly. "*Ya v skuchnye!*"

Her Russian was idomatic, but its meaning was emphatic: "I am in boredom."

"Aw, shucks," my friend said, having feared the worst. "What you need is a little relaxation. There's that new movie about Glinka everybody says is good; maybe that would help. Why don't you go see it?"

"I did," the girl said drearily. "It bores me worse."

Chapter IX

EDUCATION

THE COMMUNIST PARTY approach to education, like its approach to nearly everything, is based on a bromide by Stalin. "People," he said, "must be grown carefully and tenderly, just as a gardener grows a favorite tree."

For once, Stalin hit upon an apt simile. The new man Communism still thinks it must produce, is most likely to be produced by schooling, and if he does one day emerge he will bear the same comparison to the rest of us that the pruned and tortured espalier apple tree on the garden wall bears to the ordinary apple in the orchard. But the production of that new man remains the object of Soviet education.

There have, however, been some notable twists in Soviet ideas about how this aim is to be achieved. For some years following the revolution, Soviet educators had sought to pattern elementary and intermediate education on a system roughly similar to what, in the United States, is known as the Dalton plan. This and kindred approaches to education was a product of revolt against the harshness and rigidity of the older method of trying to inject the three Rs into the human consciousness with a hickory stick. The newer methods seek to foster mental growth by encouraging the widest possible freedom of individual development. But to the Communist party it became apparent, perhaps belatedly, that such an educational method was most likely to produce a new man who would be in direct opposition to the new state. For, while the educational system encouraged freedom and initiative — within limits — the state had set a course which would constantly narrow the limits of both.

By 1934, Stalin had reached the point where he had to start rewriting history or run the risk that even the school children of his own country would begin to see him as an ogre whose lust for power outweighed all other considerations. Hence, a decree of the Central Committee ordered the preparation of new history texts for all Soviet schools. Stalin himself, with the aid of Zhdanov and Kirov, both now dead, corrected and criticized outlines for new texts submitted by various teachers and pedagogical institutes and these now serve as the basic guides for all Soviet historians.

The kind of history that Stalin wants is best demonstrated by the *History of the Communist Party (Bolsheviks) of the Soviet Union*, popularly known as the *Short Course*, which was authorized by the Central Committee in 1938. It has since been translated into at least half a hundred languages and at the last published reckoning more than 60,000,000 copies had been distributed. In my opinion, this book is as important to the world at large as was Hitler's *Mein Kampf* but it is many times harder to read and to understand. In it, the distortions and falsifications of history are so numerous, tortuous and baldly conceived that in order to understand it fully a person needs to check nearly every page and line against original sources. Two paragraphs, however, will help to illustrate the immensity of its falsifications. On page 347, the *Short Course* states:

> "The trials showed [the reference is to the 1937 purge trials] that these dregs of humanity, in conjunction with the enemies of the people Trotsky, Zinoviev and Kamenev, had been in conspiracy against Lenin, the party, and the Soviet

state ever since the early days of the October Socialist Revolution. The insidious attempts to thwart the peace of Brest-Litovsk at the beginning of 1918, the plot against Lenin* and the conspiracy with the 'left' Socialist-Revolutionaries for the arrest and murder of Lenin, Stalin and Sverdlov in the spring of 1918, the villainous shot that wounded Lenin in the summer of 1918, the revolt of the 'left' Socialist-Revolutionaries in the summer of 1918, the deliberate aggravation of differences in the party in 1921 with the object of undermining and overthrowing Lenin's leadership from within, the attempts to overthrow the party leadership during Lenin's illness and after his death, the betrayal of state secrets and the supply of information of an espionage character to foreign espionage services, the vile assassination of Kirov, the acts of wrecking, diversion and explosions, the dastardly murder of Menzhinsky, Kuibyshev and Gorky — all these and similar villainies over a period of twenty years were committed, it transpired, with the participation or under the direction of Trotsky, Zinoviev, Kamenev, Rykov and their henchmen, at the behest of espionage services of the bourgeois states."

In order to believe this it is necessary to believe that from the inception of the Soviet state until 1937 all of its leaders except Lenin and Stalin and a small handful of Stalin's henchmen were agents of German espionage. Again the *Short Course* tells us that in April of 1917 Lenin criticized Kamenev and "some of the old Bolsheviks" for clinging to the old formula of a revolutionary democratic dictatorship — but omits to mention that Stalin himself, as one of the editors of *Pravda*, was aligned with Kamenev at that time.

As these two illustrations suggest the *Short Course* is a

---

* On August 30, 1918, a woman named Fanya Kaplan shot and severely wounded Lenin because, she said, he was a traitor to the revolution.

compound of falsities, and not even skilfully contrived. It is not history, but rather an ex parte justification of Stalin's course in shooting all the top-ranking Bolsheviks who might have challenged his power or opposed his decisions, while, at the same time, it represents Stalin as a lonely giant on a pedestal of infallibility.

But it is also the cornerstone of Soviet education, dedicated, in its introduction, to strengthening "our certainty of the ultimate victory of the great cause of the party of Lenin-Stalin, the victory of Communism throughout the world."

Educational reforms which Stalin and the party initiated with the revision of history in 1934 have proceeded in spasmodic waves. In 1943, for example, coeducation in elementary and intermediate schools was abolished, not because of any prudish scruples but because of problems of discipline and chiefly, to quote a Soviet textbook for teachers called *Pedagogy*, published in 1946, "by the necessity of differentiating in the work of military-physical preparation of the youth of the two sexes." Segregation, in short, was a wartime measure which the party hierarchy decided to carry over into peace.

To judge from Soviet newspaper articles written by Soviet educators, discipline is an apparently increasing problem. Two newspaper articles show what is being done.

The first is by one Apnautev, described as assistant head of the Moscow city department of national education, and it begins with the ominous warning: "If children break the rules for behavior in public places and on streets parents will be fined, and even charged with criminal responsibility."

Then, turning to schools, it continues: "The Soviet school must be distinguished from any other school primarily by its strict discipline, because the higher the human society for which the school is preparing young people, the firmer discipline must be. The regulations for Suvorov schools [junior military academies], where punishment goes as far as detention cells, have been accepted by the teachers. If firm discipline is sought in ordinary schools, there must also be firm order.

"It is not necessary to work out a complete system of punishment. The question of the forms of punishment can be left to the teacher. Punishment must be reasonable and justified. For inattentiveness in lessons the pupil can be sent out of the room. But it would be better to put the pupil in a corner of the classroom where he would at least hear the lesson and not run about the corridors interfering with the work of other classes. If the pupil breaks the sanitary rules by dirtying the classrooms it would be wisest to make him clean the room. Such forms of punishment will be reasonable and justified.

"For hooliganism children can be expelled from school. But it would be more consistent to send the pupil to the labor education colony where he would go through a new and more severe school and one which would perhaps be useful to him. Those kind of people who want to make the labor educational colonies more interesting by means of games and working circles are wrong. Special children's rooms attached to police stations have become too much like clubs. Children who behave like hooligans are willing to go there because they find table games and good conversationalists, or, as they are called, pedagogical workers.

It should be recommended to the police that they should be police and not pedagogues so that young people who have been sent to a children's room will not want to go there again.

"People who say that children misbehave because they have nothing to do are wrong. These people think that in order to keep children well behaved they must be occupied and amused by all kinds of interesting shows. This develops in children neither character nor consciousness of duty, nor habits of work. In life people have to do other things besides interesting things. Every person has his duty which he must fulfill. Why do children have so much free time? Why do they not put in their time carrying out all the homework the teacher has set? Even capable children have to put in a good deal of time to learn their lessons properly and less capable ones even more."

The second article, by the woman director of a girls' school, deals with girls exclusively: "We are in no way trying to turn our girls into 'ladies in muslin.' The task of the girls' schools is to form and bring up bold and work-loving patriots ready to do great things in their country's name. The girls' schools must bring into being girls who are equipped for useful work and useful social activity and who have access to any profession. But at the same time the school must make the girls good members of the family, loving and capable mothers, and bringers-up of children.

"Whilst the girls' schools must give the same profound and many-sided scientific teaching as boys' schools, they must also develop in the girls femininity, modesty and a feeling of great worthiness and honor of women. They must teach the girls how to think, how to work with books, and must at the same time give them a whole series of practical habits which are necessary to life in the family. We must remember all the time that the future of our country depends on how we bring up our girls because they are the mothers of the future.

"In this school we are now setting aside one hour a week when the class leader explains to the girls what discipline is, what the principles of morals and politeness are, how to behave towards adults and children, how to behave in social places, etc. The teachers are developing in the girls a taste for everything beautiful. They are trying to make the school such that the girls will love it and make it comfortable and attractive by their own efforts. Our naturalists' circle has provided almost all the classes with flowers, and halls and corridors are hung with pictures and portraits many of them painted by the pupils. In the reading room and other common rooms the tablecloth and curtains are also made by the girls. The pupils clean the classrooms in turn.

"We can already see developing (six months after segregation) the outward appearance which ought to belong to a member of a girls' school. We are advising our girls to wear their hair straight in plaits and are teaching them to be tidy. In the junior classes there is a 'tidiness corner' with needles, thread, soap and towels. If a girl comes to school in torn clothes it is suggested that she should mend them or, which is even more effective, it is suggested that other pupils help her. And, as the girls have plenty of self-respect the needles and thread from the tidiness corner are now scarcely made use of. The girls mend their own torn clothes at home.

"Housekeeping is being taught in a school circle, and during holidays girls of senior classes have arranged a dressmaking evening and have made dresses for themselves."

Taken together these two articles spell out the method now in use to reach one goal of Soviet education which was defined in *Komsomolskaya Pravda*, the newspaper of the Young Communist League. It said: "In the Soviet school education must be conducted on a basis of a correct combination between methods of persuasion and the need for the complete fulfillment by school children of established rules and order in and out of school." Which is merely another way of saying that the elementary school is the place to bring home to future Soviet workers and leaders the meaning of Vishinsky's definition of the Soviet state as a "welding of persuasion and coercion."

Structurally, the Soviet education system takes this form:

Kindergartens — for children three to six and as yet coeducational.

Elementary [sometimes also called primary], schools consisting of eight forms — for children seven through fourteen years of age and segregated. Formerly the entering age was eight and these schools had seven forms. They were thus called *Semletki*, or seven-year schools, and the name is still popularly used to designate them.

Middle School — Three forms for ages fifteen, sixteen and seventeen and also segregated.

Higher education — Universities and polytechnical institutes.

Additionally there are three types of schools which do

not fit into any of these catagories and demand more extensive description. They are:

Industrial Schools — These are in three groups; trade
schools, factory and plant training called the FZO schools,
and schools for the training of railway workers. The place
of importance accorded these institutions in the Soviet
scheme was indicated by Stalin in 1939 when he called for
an annual transfer of 1,500,000 young people from farms to
urban factories. The figure has never been achieved, but it
is estimated that such schools currently have an annual
total enrollment of around 500,000 boys and *girls.*

Enrollment is partly voluntary and partly coercive. Backward children in the ordinary schools are sometimes com-
pulsorily transferred to industrial schools at the age of fourteen, against their own or even their parents' wishes.
Delinquents are enrolled by police agencies. Annual quotas
are set by government decree and enforced by party, government and trade-union committees, and the process
referred to in such military terms as "call-up" or "mobilization."

In an article which was at once exhortatory and explana-
tory, *Pravda* (September 10, 1944) said: "In the oblasts
[regions] of Omsk, Saratov, Chelyabinsk, Yaroslavl and
Gorky the mobilization and medical commissions have not
been organized. The quotas to be fulfilled in each district
have not been fixed, and the readiness of the schools to
receive youths have not been checked. The reason is that
the responsible officials look upon the call-up as an affair of
secondary importance. The mobilization commissions must
not permit the recurrences of such malpractices as the
enrollment of youths who are under the minimum age, or

are not physically fit. The chairmen of the executive committees of town and district soviets are directly responsible
for the work of mobilization commissions."

School conditions are sometimes execrable. Concerning
School Number One in the Istyinsky machine-tool factory,
Komsomolskaya Pravda reported: "Last year the school
was not heated. Not a single machine tool was assigned for
the training of turners. Special clothing was not provided
for the foundry workers. They were not even given gloves
for work connected with the shaping of moulds. There was
no electric light in the dormitories. Owing to the shortage
of fuel the pupils got baths at irregular intervals. A dining
room intended for 40 has to accomodate hundreds and
rations were not received in full."

But in *Izvestiya* a factory director boasted that he had
speeded up the tempo of education by new methods. Pupils, he said, "went to workshops in marching formations.
They were first trained how to stand at the machines, and
how to hold tools. After a month, they were allowed to
work independently. They received six hours of practical,
two hours of theoretical, and one hour of political training
daily." By theoretical training, it is assumed he meant the
three Rs, because the stated function of the schools is to
provide an equivalent of seven-year education while teaching a trade. Political training, as in all Soviet education, is
based upon Stalin's *Short Course*.

Suvorov and Nakhimov Schools — These institutions,
already mentioned as places where detention cells have
been approved as a method of punishment, are ten-year
military schools for boys aged eight to eighteen. Their function is to train officers, the Suvorov schools for the army, the

Nakhimov schools for the navy. They are another wartime innovation which has been carried over into peace.

The Suvorov and Nakhimov schools seem to have been filled, at least in part, with war orphans, but if they are to continue indefinitely, as seems likely, children will have to come from other places than kindergartens for orphans and foundlings. Nowhere in the Soviet press did I ever see a figure for the number of boys in these schools, and inquiries made to the appropriate Soviet authorities for such figures went unanswered as did requests for a visit to one. For whatever it may be worth I can only observe that their uniforms appeared on Moscow's streets about as frequently as did those of the boys and girls of the industrial schools. *Red Star*, the army newspaper, did however once provide a picture of life in a Suvorov academy, and here it is:

Four months have passed since the Suvorov schools began working and these months have had an unusually great effect on the pupils, changing them beyond recognition not only in outward appearance but internally as well.

Large groups of Suvorovites came to Moscow for the holidays. They were disciplined, very polite, robust boys who already had a feeling for military bearing and even a certain spruceness. They are passionately interested in everything connected with the Red Army offensive, know by heart the map of the locality where the offensive is proceeding, and show tremendous interest in all kinds of present-day equipment. At the same time they are still genuine children with everything that is good in children: they chuckle at tricks of the clown in the circus, and hold their breath when seeing a fairy-tale film.

Different kinds of children entered the Suvorov schools and a good deal of teaching ability and feeling and experi-

ence as a military commander were needed to discipline
them, to establish authority among them, and to inculcate
a sense of duty and honor. But the officer-teachers have
proved equal to this task. The directorates of the Suvorov
schools succeeded in choosing people who possessed a
happy combination of pedagogic and military training.
Many of the officer-tutors and teachers have taken part in
the Patriotic War and been decorated and they are facing
their new work with enthusiasm.

The whole system of work done in the Suvorov schools
is so arranged as to make the future officer a well-educated,
physically agile and morally reliable person. The pupil's
days are fully occupied. They all get up at a bugle call
quickly and carefully complete their toilets and are then
inspected by the duty tutor-officer. They march to the
dining room for breakfast and then into the classroom
where they spend an hour getting ready for lessons. At a
given signal they begin their studies — four hours for the
younger pupils and six hours for the older ones. Little boys
in the preparatory classes are learning Russian and at the
same time are beginning to study English or German. After
their studies they have dinner, go for a walk with a band,
read, go to the workshops or busy themselves with music,
dancing and singing. In the evening they prepare lessons
for the next day, have supper and are in bed by ten o'clock.

If this description is taken as accurate, and there seems
no reason why it should not be, the life of the little officer is
idyllic compared to the life of the student factory hand,
just as in adult life.

Technicums — Essentially, these are comparable to voca-
tional high schools and turn out technically trained men
and women of a status higher than a skilled worker, and
lower than a trained engineer. *Pravda* had provided some

figures concerning the scope and shortcomings of this phase of Soviet education: "At the present time [1944] there are 2,173 technicums in the Soviet Union training 500,000 students. The disproportion between the number of technicians being trained and the demand for them is felt most seriously at the present moment. The factories of the ferrous-metal industry require 4,000 technicians but the technicums will provide only an insignificant fraction of this total. Only 25 to 30 per cent of the demands of the coal, building, and electro-technical industries will be met. In many factories there are twice as many engineers as technicians. Experience . . . shows that specialists with secondary education should be from two to three times as numerous as specialists with higher education. Hence the necessity of extending the network of technicums, and increasing the number of students in those presently existing." But in 1948 the picture remained substantially unchanged.

Such is the Soviet Union's educational network. In 1949, in all these institutions, out of a population of 190,000,000, about 30,000,000 persons are going to school. This compares to 28,000,000 out of 140,000,000 population in the United States. In the villages, schools are usually one-room affairs (as in rural United States) and many pupils never go beyond the fourth year. In the cities, a seven or eight-year education seems to be the average. University education or its technical equivalent is limited, partly by lack of facilities and partly by the system, to a total enrollment of less than 700,000, compared with 2,400,000 in American colleges, universities and polytechnics.

But the system is aimed at providing higher education

only for those who can, by their scholastic records, earn it
or for those whose families can afford it. A student proceeding from the so-called seven-year schools to the middle
school must pass entrance examinations regardless of the
marks he or she has made, and the same applies to those
progressing from the middle schools to the universities.

Because propaganda claims conflict with other official
statements it is impossible to determine the amount of
illiteracy, and the general level of education.

In 1939, a Soviet General, M. Antonov, analyzed the military class called up that year as follows: Ten per cent had
intermediate or higher schooling; 65 per cent had seven-
year schooling and 25 per cent three to five years. In 1939,
the call-up age was abruptly dropped from 22 years to 19,
which meant that three age classes were called up at once.
Since the call-up is universal, the figures ought to indicate
how universal Soviet education is as well as how far many
students go. But they obviously did not do so. In subsequent exhortatory admonitions to party workers in the Red
Army, instructions to read newspapers and communiqués
to illiterate men, as well as party orders to cultivate their
good will by writing letters for them, were prominent.

Another, less reliable but more interesting index was
offered by the ex-chief of Propaganda and Agitation,
Georgi F. Alexandrov. He said: "The party now counts
more than 6 million in its ranks. The finest Soviet intellectuals have been drawn into the party. It now has more than
400,000 with higher education, and 1,340,000 with secondary education. It has 148,000 engineers, 24,000 agronomists,
40,000 doctors and 80,000 teachers." When these figures are
turned upside down, the big fact that emerges is that two

out of three Communist party members did not get more than a seven-year education.

In the elementary and middle years, Soviet education seems far more intensive than in the United States. A 1945 educational directive provided: "History, natural science and geography as independent subjects will in the future be taught from the fourth instead of the third forms. In the first three forms pupils will be given information on history, natural science and geography during the reading lesson.

"The basic subjects in the first three forms will be Russian and arithmetic, and fourteen hours per week will be devoted to each. In arithmetic, there is no change in the syllabus of the junior forms. In the fourth form more attention will be paid to decimals, whereas ordinary fractions and the divisibility of figures will be studied more closely in the fifth form. The new syllabus pays greater attention to the solution of mathematical problems, which tends to develop logical lines of thought. Elementary geography will be taught in the second and third forms during the reading lesson. The importance of observation and practical experience is stressed; all formality [in Soviet language formality means among other things teaching, and reciting, by rote] should be eliminated from the study of geography."

The emphasis of this directive on arithmetic and geography will be better understood in the light of two paragraphs from *Pedagogy*:* The paragraphs: "In the course on geography attention should be given to the development of the ability to define the cardinal points, to use the compass, to understand a topographical plan, to read a

* For specialists a great deal more of this book is available in a translation by Professor George S. Counts and Mrs. Nucia P. Dodge, called *I Want to be Like Stalin*. John Day Co., 1947.

map, to grasp the relations of the various elements of relief. This is an essential part of military study.

"Mathematics should provide training in the use of the scale, the divider, the caliper and other instruments in the making of a simple survey of a locality. Knowledge of mathematics is extremely important for the mastery of military technique."

To round out this picture, I think it will be necessary to introduce a Soviet child I knew, and tell something of her return to school after a summer vacation. Purely for purposes of concealing her identity we will call her Vera. She was merely one of millions.

To fourteen-year-old Vera, going back to school was an adventure that came every year. Some weeks before school reopened, Vera reminded her parents that she would need lots of books, different from the ones she had used the preceding year. Vera was going to be in the seventh form.

It was very important for Vera to make good marks this year, although she always had. In the Soviet system of grading pupils, figures are used. Five stands for excellent, four for good, three for passing and so on. If Vera failed to get fours and fives she might be transferred to a trade school, and thus lose her chance of eventually attending a university, which was her ambition. But her goal was a report card of "all fives," and to get that it was very important to have all her own books. For, if she had to share some of her books with classmates — which had happened to her before and which many children had to do because of the chronic shortage of textbooks — the opportunity of getting her homework done properly would be that much diminished.

Altogether, Vera needed fifteen books, not counting her notebooks. The newspapers had said that, in preparation for the new school year, 40 million new textbooks had been printed and that sounded like a lot. But it was millions short of being enough to go round, and Vera did not expect to have any new books at all. She would be satisfied with secondhand ones, and so, helped by her mother and father, she began looking for them weeks before school actually opened.

In the free market she found some of the necessary books, paying in one instance 60 roubles for a book which had sold for two when it was new. Finding all the books was both exciting and costly, but when school opened, she was fully equipped. Altogether, her books cost the equivalent of what her father earned in a month.

The school to which Vera reported was a fifteen-minute trolley ride from her home. The school operated in two shifts because there were not enough schools to take care of all the children in Moscow on a one-shift day. Vera's classes were in the morning. The school was a largish, four-story building with big windows and wide, freshly scrubbed corridors. On the walls were many pictures of Stalin and Lenin, and a few of Marx and Engels with their big white beards. There were other pictures, showing children washing their teeth, or combing their hair, other children playing volleyball or doing calisthenics, and pictures of earnest, studious children hard at work in their classrooms. In addition to the classrooms, the school contained a big recreation room, a teachers room, a chemistry lab and a physics lab. In the whole school there were upwards of 400 children in each shift, and except when they went to the labs, or during recess, each class stayed in the same room, with different teachers coming in for forty-minute work periods. In the one building there were children from seven to seventeen.

There was also a buffet for lunches, but Vera could not buy her lunch every day. A lunch consisting of a piece of sausage on a slab of bread, and a small piece of candy, cost three roubles, or 72 roubles a month. Vera's father and mother could not afford this much.

In the seventh form Vera would study algebra, plane geometry, physics, chemistry, Soviet history, Russian literature, economic geography of the Soviet Union and English. The heavy load and the short school day made Vera's homework larger and longer than it would have been if there had been more schools in Moscow. But Vera did not know this. She only knew that she had a lot of work to do.

This was to be Vera's year of real acquaintance with the *Short Course*. She had had it in a rudimentary way in the fourth form, but this year its study would begin in earnest. In fact, her schedule was pretty heavily loaded with subjects concerning the Soviet Union. In the sixth form she had been given a Communist view of the world outside. This is what her geography study told her about the United States:

"The huge wealth of that country is in the hands of capitalist-industrialist trusts — steel, oil, copper, etc. Having at their disposal hundreds of billions of dollars, the millionaires lead a luxurious life and sweat the workers as hard as they can. The working day lasts from nine to ten hours. The labor of American workers is more intensive than in Europe. At the age of 45, the worker loses his health and becomes an old man.

"The world crisis has badly hit American industry. Thousands of factories have shut down and millions of workers have been thrown out on the streets. In 1934, the U.S. had 17,000,000 unemployed. Unemployment reached dimensions never before seen in other countries. In the very center of New York the unemployed evicted from their quarters lived in old boxes resembling dog kennels. Half naked and starved they searched for food in garbage cans. [This would have a particularly horrible connotation for a Soviet child, since Soviet garbage cans never contain anything even remotely edible.]

"In cultural matters the U.S. is besieged by contrasts. There are a few schools organized by American million-aires which are luxuriously equipped and rich in all kinds of equipment. In contrast the schools for the masses are poor and frequently in one room with one teacher there are three classes."

But there are other angles to Soviet education and one of them is shown by this cable I sent to *Time* magazine from Moscow:

In *Komsomolskaya Pravda* this week there appears an article by one N. Katkov, secretary of the Chapayev City Committee of the Communist Party on "The duty of party organizations to see to it that all instruction given in the schools shall be on a high ideological plane."

This article states that as a result of visits to the schools of Chapayev the party organization there had found "that teaching even of such subjects as literature, history and geography was at times conducted in a formal manner and valuable opportunities for giving the pupils a materialistic outlook upon the world were wasted. This was particularly noticeable in the teaching of natural science and biology where the teachers had a chance of helping the pupils to develop strong and clear atheistical views."

The situation in Chapayev is another and more recent manifestation of a Soviet problem which was more clearly defined in an exchange of letters between a Komsomol group in the Vesyegonsk middle school of the Kalinin district and the editors of the magazine *Young Bolshevik*. Komsomols at Vesyegonsk wrote: "Recently in our Komsomol organization there arose a question about the attitude of Komsomol members towards religion. We consider that a Komsomol member should not believe in God or go to church and discussed this matter at a general Komsomol meeting at school. This meeting decided that a Komsomol member must not go to church. Some members disobeyed this decision. Hot discussions followed. The members who went to church referred to the law on freedom of conscience and religion and argued that they were right and the decision of the Komsomol organization was wrong. We ask you to give us your opinion on this problem."

The editors replied: "In order to answer this question it is necessary first to understand the attitude of the Communist party toward religion.

"The Communist party has always proclaimed freedom of conscience, i.e., the right of every citizen to choose the religion he likes or not to believe at all. The party has also insisted on the separation of the church from the state and school. The church no longer receives a subsidy from the state and we have no state religion. In Article 124 of the Soviet Constitution it is said: 'In order to insure to citizens the freedom of conscience, the church in the Soviet Union is separated from state and school. Freedom of religious worship and freedom of anti-religious propaganda is recognized for all citizens.'

"But this does not mean that the Communist party is indifferent to the attitude of its members toward religion. Our party considers that religion is the private business of the state but not of the Marxist working class party.

"All activity of the Communist party is based on the most advanced revolutionary doctrine of Marxism-Leninism.The theoretical base of the Communist party is dialectic materialism. This scientific attitude is incompatible with religion. Our concept is based on science. Religious doctrine is contrary to science.

"The Komsomol unites the most advanced, conscientious part of Soviet youth and for Komsomols religion is not a private business. If a Komsomol believes in God and goes to church it means he is not fulfilling his duty to the Komsomol."

By which we see that although the Soviet Constitution guarantees freedom of worship and conscience, in the very institutions where it is studied, a large segment of Soviet children are also told that the guaranty is null and void.

Chapter X

WHETHER the one child in forty who gets through a university or its technical equivalent emerges as teacher, scientist, writer, artist, actor, singer, musician or philosopher, he or she is automatically a member of the intellectual class, and a line soldier on the culture front.

In the classless society's new class structure, the intellectuals are near the apex, just beneath the approximate one per cent composed of the higher-ranking political and military personnel who make up the top strata. The intellectual class roughly equals about two and a half per cent of the population. The service demanded of intellectuals consists of a constant revision and reinterpretation of the whole of history, human experience and mankind's cumulative knowledge to prove the correctness of Marx's theories, Lenin's tactics and Stalin's infallibility. Their task is to convince the lower-classed 96 and one half per cent of the people that the Communist party system is the most advanced and enlightened in history. In essence their assignment is an order to create a culture for the new Communist man.

Like the word plan, the word culture embraces nearly everything. It is used to describe the arts and sciences from alphabet to zoology, but it is also used to designate the desirability of knowing what the fixtures in a bathroom are for, or of listening to an agitator's talk in a Red Corner. The arts and sciences are required, in fact, to serve as the hand-maidens of the half-literate agitators.

As a class, the intellectuals are highly paid compared to what most others get for their labors. Some of them, and particularly the more highly approved writers, musicians, actors, singers and, of late, the scientists, live pretty well by the standards of any country just as do the members of the Politburo. They have town apartments, country houses, cars and special stores where they can buy the best of whatever is going.

But if the rewards are high, the dangers are great. No other class has contributed as high a proportion of its numbers to the slave-labor camps. The more education an intellectual gets, the more apparent become the falsities and shams which are an integral part of the Communist power. He knows what he must do in order to play safe, but sometimes his conscience and his knowledge cause him to do things which are contrary to his instructions. Stalin, knowing this, distrusts intellectuals as a class. He, and his police, keep a wary, watchful eye on all their doings, ready to pounce at the first sign of independence. If an intellectual, whether novelist, composer, historian, economist or biologist, truckles under and faithfully executes the directives of the Politburo, he knows he will be fed and despised. But if he does not, he knows he will be in trouble. No group in the Soviet Union is so conscious of economic and political captivity, or so poignantly imprisoned.

Once, one of my colleagues in Moscow came across a name in a newspaper item which he needed to identify further. He looked in his files and could not find it. Exasperated, he exclaimed: "why don't these people have something like a *Who's Who* where a man could find their full names and something about them?" His secretary, a university graduate, muttered half audibly, "Because they'd have to change it too often." My friend turned quickly around to join in what he thought would be her laughter. But instead he found her as intent at her typewriter as if she had not spoken, her lower lip clutched tightly between her teeth.

When they dare, Muscovites tell a wry joke. They say that Krasnoyarsk, a Siberian slave-camp center, must be the intellectual capital of the world because so many Soviet intellectuals have been sent there.

One of the instruments Stalin uses to direct and reward his stable of creative artists and scientists is the annual disbursement of the Stalin prizes. These are given for accomplishment in all intellectual fields and sometimes even when there is no accomplishment. In 1949, two architects won prizes for skyscrapers which had not yet come off their drawing boards.

The prizes range from 200,000 roubles down to as little as 25,000 and the number of prizes in any year is uncertain. In 1949, for example, 302 prizes worth 21 million roubles were handed out, compared to 242 prizes worth 18 million roubles in the preceding year.

It is not in the roubles distributed, however, but in the nature of the work for which prizes are given that the incentive quality of the awards are most apparent. Soviet writers, to be successful, must follow one of these three courses: 1) works which glorify Stalin and the Communist state; 2) works which serve as a spur to the speed-up by making labor seem heroic; 3) works which depict, as the most depraved, malicious, conniving and dangerous things ever, the governments, diplomats and businessmen of the United States and Great Britain. In general, the works of the first two groups are overstrained, unrealistic, false and artistically bad as are those of the third.

A partial list of the 1949 Stalin prizes serves to make the method more explicit. Among novels, a prize went to one Vasily Azhaev for a story about the construction of a Soviet oil pipe line and another to Semyon Babayevski for a story about a war hero who, after a great struggle with his soul, persuaded himself to return to his collective farm and take up his drudgery where he had left off. Another prize-winning novel was Tikon Semushkin's story of the evil rapacity of an American who obtained a business concession in Russia during the days of Lenin's New Economic Policy.

In poetry, Konstantin Simonov won a first prize for a volume of verse which compared life in the Soviet Union to that in the United States, which he had visited as an official guest. The United States came off very badly. A second prize was given the verses of one Mikola Bazhan, who exposed the nefarious workings of the British Labor government, which, like capitalists of the United States, is apparently grinding people into depths of soulless poverty.

In drama, prize winners included a play by Nikolai Virta which showed how a virtuous Soviet official foiled a scheming American diplomat who plotted revolution in one of the Soviet satellite states and a play for small children, called *Little Snowball*, about race discrimination in the United States.

Among artists, prize winners were those who had

painted pictures of Stalin. Among scientists, a top prize went to a nuclear physicist named Georgi Latishev for "discoveries" in atomic structure which, to judge from the meagre description of the work made public, had been largely accomplished years before by Denmark's Niels Bohr and Britain's Lord Ernest Rutherford.

Since these are the things Soviet writers must write, it is not an accident that Soviet literature has produced only one really distinguished novel since the Bolshevik coup. The novel is Mikhail Sholokov's *Tikhii Don* (The Quiet Don) which is familiar in English translations as *And Quiet Flows the Don*. It is about a Cossack family that lived in a village on the River Don, the village boys who went to World War I, the revolution, then the Bolsheviks who came dividing brother against brother and, in the village, family against family. The thing which lends this book its distinction is the artistic detachment of the author. It is not totally devoid of Communist propaganda, but the propaganda is not obtrusive. Sholokov succeeds in making the reader feel that he is not intent on proving anything, but simply in showing what happened, how and why. Because of the detachment, the book achieves a kind of integrity which is missing from most Soviet literature and art.

Sholokov's novel was published a number of years ago, and he has not since followed it with anything noteworthy. He lives far from Moscow, shuns the capital as much as possible, is conspicuously absent from the wrangles and semi-public soul searchings of the Soviet Writer's Union, and he has probably been having difficulty getting his subsequent writing past the censor. It is likely that *Tikhii Don* itself could not now get past the censors. For it does not

blatantly enough reflect *Pravda's* instructional dictum that
"the principle of party spirit is the main principle of Soviet
literature and art." As time has passed, the internal Soviet
censorship and thought control has become more and more
insistent that all Soviet art forms fulfill this test.

Stalin himself put it more bluntly when he launched the
postwar purge of Soviet arts and sciences. Assembling the
Central Committee, Stalin paced the floor while Alexandrov, then head of Agitation and Propaganda, read off
the charges. The targets were Mikhail Zoschenko, a short-
story writer, and Anna Akhmatova, a poet. Zoschenko, said
Alexandrov in effect, was writing stuff which made the
glorious Soviet citizen seem like a monkey in a zoo. "It is
time," responded Stalin in his lethally calm way, "this man
decided if he is for us or against us."

Zoschenko is one of the most capable writers in Russia
today. He is a satirist, a sort of Russian Ring Lardner whose
stories seem funny as they go down line by line and then,
at the end, explode with the shattering surprise of a booby
trap.

A typical Zoschenko story concerns the peasant boy who
went off to the city and got a job in an airplane factory.
After a time he decided to return to the village for a vacation. The factory's party agitator extracted a promise that,
when he got home, he would make an agitation for the
airplane.

In due course the collective chairman ordered the village
people to gather, and hear the agitation for the airplane.
The audience stayed glum and totally disinterested until,
inadvertently the speaker mentioned the awful destruction
that followed upon a crash, at which they perked up. When

an airplane fell did the people in it get killed? Did they?
And how! Stimulated the returnee told tale after tale, each
more terribly destructive than the last about what an airplane could do to people who crashed in them.The peasants
were getting more and more enthusiastic when one had a
horrible thought. Did an airplane kill cows? Did it? Still
more stimulated the returnee told of teats and horns scattered over an acre when an airplane propeller chopped up
a cow. And horses? Horses, too. Now the peasant faces
began to glower, and angry muttering filled the village
clubhouse. What, the chairman wanted to know, should a
collective village do about the airplane? Why, the speaker
responded, they should all chip in and buy one. Whereat
the peasants filed out in dumb defiant anger. The airplane,
quite plainly, was a new Moscow plot against their cows.

For stories like this, Zoschenko was deprived of his
writing livelihood. Many people felt that he had been lucky
to get off so lightly.

Zoschenko's particular genius is his subtle, aloof, low-
keyed laughter. If his agitator is ridiculous, so is the whole
system of agitation, as witness the real-life instance of the
agitator who addressed his audience in a language they
could not understand. To agitate for the airplane to a group
of peasants who know the value of a cow and reject as
absurd the notion that a man should try to make a bird of
himself, is ridiculous too, but it is also a phase of activity
that goes on every day everywhere in the Communist party
system. To this degree Zoschenko is a writer who lampoons
the society in which he lives — a social critic. In the Communist party system this is not only not funny, it is intol-
erable. Hence a man like Zoschenko must be suppressed.

Anna Akhmatova was a totally different case. Born in 1893, she published her first slim volume of poetry called *The Evening* in 1911, and followed it up with others until, by 1922, she had gotten six out. The titles are suggestive: *The Rosary, The White Flock, The Plantain, Anno Domini: MCMXXI.*

In 1913 she and her husband, Nikolai Gumilyov, founded a literary movement called the "acmeists," the aim of which was to renounce mystical images in Russian literature and replace them with clear, definite ones; to recognize the artistic self-value of every event in life; to use every word with absolute precision. This sort of thing would have been pretty precious stuff in any proletarian society. Whether because of it, or some other crime, the Bolsheviks executed her husband in 1921, but by that time they had been divorced.

Whether Akhmatova had read John Donne is doubtful, but in her poetry she made a real effort to capture something of the thing Donne meant when he wrote: "But, because Angels could not propagate, nor make more Angels, he enlarged his love in making man so that he might enjoy all natures at once and have the nature of earthly Creatures in one Person."

After the middle twenties she ceased to write at all, and still, throughout the thirties, her stuff was adored by girl university students. After war began, she resumed writing and was published in a Leningrad magazine called *Zvezda* (Star), which led to her receiving her comeuppance. The Central Committee sentenced her to the same literary darkness to which Zoschenko was sent because "she is full of pessimism and decadence, without ideas and full of mysticism, and calculated to do harm to the education of Soviet youth."

It is worth while to suggest some of the things that might have happened had the United States maintained such a system during the past thirty years. John Dos Passos, John Steinbeck, William Faulkner, Erskine Caldwell, Ernest Hemingway and a host of less competent craftsmen could never have published most of what they wrote. Nor could Elinor Wylie, Edna St. Vincent Millay, or Willa Cather. In the cases of Dos Passos, Steinbeck, Faulkner and Caldwell the simple act of submission of their books to the censorship board would have resulted in police action against them.

But the operation of such supervision does more than simply dispose of stillborn books, plays and poetry. It also degrades the artist as a man, and perverts his talent as an artist. Now in his seventies, Kornei Chukovsky is a tall, sad, silent man with a shock of gray hair and a considerable talent for verse. Many years ago, before the revolution, Chukovsky came by accident upon Walt Whitman's *Leaves of Grass.* He was fired with enthusiasm. He translated Whitman into Russian, and began a long, one-man crusade to bring the American apostle of brotherhood to the Russian people. There was something about Whitman that struck the Czar's police as subversive and Chukovsky was muzzled by threats of Siberia. But he went on being Whitman's admirer, disciple and proselytizer and after the revolution succeeded in getting out a volume of Whitman translations. Yet, the day came when Whitman got Chukovsky into as much trouble with the Communists as he had with the Czars. The result is that Chukovsky nowadays pours his talent into verse which encourages children to keep their teeth brushed and their hair combed.

It is almost as if Whitman had Chukovsky in mind when he wrote:

> Oh Christ! This is mastering me!
> In at the conquer'd doors they crowd. I am possess'd. . . .
> Enough! Enough! Enough!
> Somehow I have been stunn'd. Stand back!
> Give me a little time beyond my cuff'd head, slumbers,
>   dreams, gaping;
> I discover myself on the verge of a usual mistake.

The postwar arts purge was touched off more by general circumstances than by any single event. During the fighting, the Kremlin hierarchy had been preoccupied; it had little or no time to devote to the tasks of cultural arbiter. In many fields, and especially in the arts, many Soviet people misunderstood this preoccupation. They mistook it for the glimmer of a new day, a new freedom, a slight but perceptible step towards emancipation of the creative mind, and they acted accordingly. When the Kremlin did get around to action, it had to act with enough vigor and ruthlessness to emphasize its return to the *status quo ante*.

One symptom of the general mistake, and one which helped precipitate Kremlin action, was the production by the Moscow Art Theatre of Oscar Wilde's *An Ideal Husband*. When it was written, Wilde's play was simply an evening's entertainment provided mainly by its bright dialogue. The Art Theatre decided to play it that way. But even Moscow's critics, who had generally fallen into the habit of praising anything the controlling Arts Committee permitted to be produced, saw the error of this one. For the Art Theatre's actors and actresses, being technically excellent, played Wilde so straight, the horrified critics reported, that "bourgeois decadence" seemed to justify itself. Hence, the theatre also needed a purge.

A look at the list of plays the Moscow theatres were offering at that period is enough to show what, from the Kremlin's view, was wrong. In Moscow's 29 palaces of culture — the figure includes two opera and ballet theatres, three puppet theatres, two concert halls for serious music, a Jewish theatre, a Gypsy theatre and the circus, but not the 40 motion-picture houses — the three most popular shows were Somerset Maugham's *The Circle,* Wilde's play, and Chekhov's *Three Sisters.* There was only one modern Soviet play, a drab and uninspired piece about an American businessman who visited Moscow and had the scales removed from his eyes, and one American play, Lillian Hellman's *The Little Foxes.* The rest were pre-revolutionary Russian mediocrities which, having been of a neutral shade when written, remained neutral, and therefore contributed little to the theatre's job of glorifying Communism and vilifying its "enemies." The Soviet theatre was obviously guilty of dereliction.

When the Kremlin barked, several things were done to correct this situation. Foreign plays, except that of Miss Hellman, were wiped off the boards overnight, and a number of additional ones in rehearsal at the time abandoned. One Prudkin, the party organizer at the Art Theatre, reported that he had instituted a system of holding individual conversations with members of the theatre's company "to familiarize ourselves more closely with the political literacy of the individual members," and had "organized study groups to study the *Short Course*. He added: "No intuition, no artistic sensitivity will aid the creative worker if he is not armed with Marxist-Leninist theory."

Soviet writers, of course, tried to step into the breach with new plays. Most spectacular of these was Konstantin Simonov's *The Russian Question*. This was the story of an American newspaperman whose capitalist publisher sent him to Russia, promising a large sum of dollars for an anti-Soviet book. But the reporter was an honest fellow; he saw the Soviet system was okay and he wrote a book to say so. This so infuriated the publisher that he not only fired this super-courageous reporter, but set about the evil, vindictive course of wrecking his life, wife and home. Simonov's characterizations were so ill-informed and crude that even the most ardent Soviet sympathizers among Americans in Moscow gaped incredulously at the falsities he had been forced to introduce in order to make plausible theatre out of a basically spurious theme. But it won a 200,000-rouble Stalin prize and was put on in several Moscow theatres as well as some 200-odd others scattered over the Soviet Union simultaneously.

The Soviet theatre is wholly subsidized; it can be as lavish with any production as it needs to be. For this reason, the opera and ballet put on in Moscow's Bolshoy (Great) Theatre are technically superb. Looking over the repertoire of this theatre is, however, like scanning a collection of forty- and fifty-year-old playbills. Nearly everything put on now, was new then. Exceptions are Sergei Prokofiev's *Romeo and Juliet* (written in 1911) and his *Cinderella*, written since his return to the Soviet Union in

1933. But in these Prokofiev, like the Bolshoy, has played safe by adhering closely to the classical.

His more experimental new opera *War and Peace,* based on Tolstoy's novel, has had innumerable censor and production troubles and Prokofiev, like his colleagues, Dmitri Shostakovich and Aram Khatchaturian, has been under the fire of the Communist party purists. Even so, his *Romeo and Juliet,* as staged at the Bolshoy Theatre, remains one of the most breathtaking theatrical experiences of my life, and the only ballet I would ever bother to see again.

When a political system which seeks to buttress its power through the rigorous enforcement of rigid dogma lays its hands upon the arts, *rigor mortis* soon follows. Nowhere on the Soviet scene is this more aptly demonstrated than in the graphic arts. Until the later years of Peter the Great (the early ones of the eighteenth century) Soviet painting was dominated by the Orthodox Church and consisted almost entirely of icons painted by monks, some of which were undeniably great. But after so late and hesitant a start, secular art never quite caught up with the West.

For a time, in the early years of the revolution, poster art, which was wholly devoted to political ends, showed a vitality and inventiveness which promised much. But it could never flower into anything more because it had to go on expressing the same ideas over and over until it became stereotyped and sterile. Artists of more ambition and talent soon learned that they had to spend so much time painting the hand that fed them that they had little energy or ambition left over for the work they might have preferred to do. The result is that there is now no painting in the Soviet Union that is worth discussing. Nor can the modelers and stonecutters who spend their time making heads, busts, and heroic casts of Lenin and Stalin qualify for inclusion in a serious discussion of anything called sculpture. Even so robust and vigorous a talent as America's sculptor Jo Davidson would probably soon tire of making heads of Lenin and Stalin from photographs.

The net result is that the best of the graphic arts in the Soviet Union now are the folk arts which survive, only a little altered, from the days of serfdom. These are the embroideries of the peasant women who, in the main, stick to the traditional designs and only occasionally work a portrait of Stalin into a tablecloth; the painters of lacquer boxes who, with a wealth of detail and a rich subtlety of coloring, cover the box lids with illustrations of fairy tales and the makers of decorative plaster figurines who fashion people and animals in shapes and colors undreamt by nature. Like Russian folk dances and folk melodies these are arts which live deeply within the people, and may survive the Communists.

The man who made the plight of the artist in the Communist system more real, poignant and terrible to me than any other was Sergei Eisenstein, the motion-picture director. Now that he is dead, he deserves a memorial wherever free artists gather, for though the system demeaned him and degraded his work it never broke his spirit. To the last he tried with courage and quiet audacity to say what he wanted to say.

I met Eisenstein in the Kremlin hospital where I went to interview him about his last picture, a never-completed trilogy about Czar Ivan the Terrible (1530-1584). At the time of this meeting, his picture had not yet received the bitter and menacing denunciation it was later given by the Central Committee. At the moment he had finished cutting the second part, Eisenstein had fallen over the cutting machine with a heart attack from which he was recovering.

He was propped up on pillows, pale, flashing his golden teeth in a welcoming grin. "I suppose," he said, "it was something of a shock to your people in America to learn that Russians are subject to the same mortal infirmities as other people. I suspect they hadn't realized that a Russian could be run to bed by a bad heart." He chuckled. "That's too bad. We should know each other better. Well, tell them that I've now begun to live a postscriptum to my life. I've no reason at all to be alive, except stubbornness."

Eisenstein was reading a book about Christ by the mystery writer Dorothy Sayers. "I've always been fascinated," he said, "by the way mystery writers seem in the end to turn to mysticism. I've an idea there is something in one that leads into the other. It's interesting to see my old friend Sayers following out my theory."

But there was more on his mind than the mysticism of Miss Sayers. There was also the mysticism of Eisenstein. "I don't know how I got through dealing with Ivan this far," he said. He accompanied this statement with a motion of his right hand, fingers waving, suggesting a man groping his way through a dark labyrinth.

Briefly he recounted a series of events which seemed to him somehow connected with Ivan. Alexei Tolstoy, a Soviet writer unrelated to the great Leo, died of heart failure while writing the third of a trilogy of plays about Ivan. Nikolai Khmelov, a distinguished Soviet actor, died of a stroke while walking on for his first scene in the first full-dress rehearsal of Tolstoy's second play about Ivan.

"I don't know how I escaped," said Eisenstein. "Perhaps it was the noise of the cutting machine that scared him away."

Behind Eisenstein's preoccupation with the spiritistic vengeance of the Terrible Ivan, there was a question which came up in the conversation not once, but several times. What would the censors do with Part II? Plainly, although his doctor had forbidden him to worry, he was worried.

A few days before, the first part of his Ivan had been shown in Paris, and the reaction of the French audience made newspaper headlines. It had been violently divided, one part reacting with wild cheers, the other with equally wild boos and hisses. Eisenstein was interested. "The first part is too slow for foreign audiences," he said. "I made it that way so the interpretation I was putting on Ivan's life would have time to sink into the consciousness of the Russian people who, naturally, are more familiar with his life, times and historical significance. At no time in the writing or shooting did I have in mind any others but our people." Then, again, "I wonder how the censors will react to Part II?"

What Eisenstein had done, in the first part, was to depict a young monarch who had come to power with a pleasant and temperate disposition and had taken to wife a pretty, gentle girl. But all around him were ugly and evil people who had been corrupted by their lust for power. They opposed Ivan in everything he sought to do and slowly but perceptibly corrupted him, too, into a person to whom power was a driving goad, the force of life itself. As Part I ended, Ivan was pushing the borders of his state further and further outward while the limits of his humanity shrank. As his power grew, so did his lust for it, and as his lust grew, so did his terribleness.

What Eisenstein originally did in the second part only a few people know. It was never shown publicly in Moscow or anywhere else in the same shape that he left it when he swooned over the cutting machine. But what the Kremlin thought of it was made known. It was denounced and withheld on the Central Committee's order, which meant Stalin's. The reason given was that Eisenstein had distorted the reality of history to make Ivan a "kind of Hamlet," a maniac cavorting within a court circle of more maniacs.

Very definitely, Stalin or someone around him had seen a painful parallel between Stalin and Eisenstein's Ivan. Was this why he had worried about the censors? Was this why his heart nearly stopped when he finished it?

The questions will never be answered. Eisenstein played the game of the Russian intellectual under the Communist thumb by the prescribed rules to the end. He confessed his error. He publicly repented and promised never to do it again. With the gesture of an irrepressible gamin, he blamed it all on his subconscious mind which, he said, having been trained in a bourgeois world, according to a bourgeois morality, quite often played mean tricks on him by obtruding into his work bourgeois sentiments while the back of his conscious mind was turned.

Like a good soldier in the battle for the new culture, he shot Part II over again to kill out the errors of his malicious subconscious and when that was done, surrendered to Ivan's ghost.

Sometimes the true spirit of the Russian artistic genius breaks through the ideological strait jacket and something genuinely good emerges. This happened at least once during the war, in a song called *Dark Night*. The melody is haunting, and minor-keyed. A soldier at the front sings to his faraway wife:

"Dark night has laid itself between us on the black steppe.
Only the bullets are whistling,
Only the wind is roaring in the wild,
And above the stars glisten in the sky.

Oh, my beloved, I know you are not sleeping,
But sitting by the cradle, silently wiping a tear,
Thinking of me.

Oh, how much I love you.
How I would like to embrace you just once.

I trust you, my dearly beloved,
And this faith saves me from the dark, and the bullets.

I am not frightened, because I know you will wait for me,
Whatever my wounds may be.

Death is not frightening,
Many times she has watched over me, on the steppe."

This song was especially popular among the intellectuals, perhaps because many of them felt a spiritual kinship with the soldier on the black steppe in the dark night.

Chapter XI

THE *Oxford Dictionary* defines the word propaganda as meaning "an association or a scheme for the propagation of a doctrine or practice," and *Roget's Thesaurus* offers as synonyms for it such words as "persuasion," "proselytism," "indoctrination," or "inoculation." Today, both the definition and the synonyms are pitifully inadequate and the degree of their inadequacy is one of the measures of what is wrong with our world, and our thinking. The truth is that we can no longer define the word and, lacking a definition, we sometimes fail to recognize propaganda when it slaps us in the face.

As it is used today, propaganda is an elusive evil. Except in the degree that Communism demands of its adherents a type of blind emotional fervor which has, in the past, been most commonly associated with some variety of religious experience, propaganda as a word has ceased to have any religious connotation. It has come to mean an instrument of politics, and particularly of power politics. It is a word which, to most of us, automatically suggests something which is vaguely deceitful. In the light of our current understanding of the word, we are instinctively aware that the skilled propagandist is one who takes cunning advantage of our optimism, credulous good will or ignorance in order to put us at a political disadvantage. Propaganda no longer seeks merely to convert; in modern usage it is more often designed to create confusion and indecision so that, in times of crisis, our ability to understand a given political situation will be frustrated and our capacity to take unified, decisive action will be thwarted.

No nation in history has ever devoted as much of its energy, brain power and resources to the maintenance of a propaganda machine as the Russian Communist party state does today. Hitler, who also developed a formidable propaganda apparatus, functioned in the belief that if a lie was made big enough, and repeated often enough, it would be believed. This became, of course, his definition of propaganda, but Lenin's definition was more subtle, more durable, and more embracing.

At the turn of the century, Lenin took up the problem of how a revolutionary party, which had as its eventual aim the seizure of power, could be constructed and kept in existence against the opposition of the Czar's police. Russia of that time did not have a free press as we now understand this term, but it did have a press that was freer than the one it now has. Lenin decided that the central core of his party must be a newspaper. In his book *What Is to be Done?*,* which is still the master textbook of tactics for Communists everywhere, he laid down a tactical axiom which has not since been changed, either in the Soviet Union or elsewhere. "A newspaper," he wrote, "is not only a collective propagandist and collective agitator, but also a collective organizer."

Upon this rock he built his temple. "In our opinion," he wrote, "the starting point of our activities, the first practical

---

* Published in many editions in the United States by the Communist-controlled International Publishers, New York, and available in any of the party bookshops.

step toward creating the organization desired, and finally the main thread following which we would be able to develop, deepen and expand that organization unswervingly, should be the establishment of a political newspaper on an all-Russian scale. . . . Without it we cannot consistently carry that all-embracing propaganda and agitation, consistent in principle, which form the chief and constant task of Social-Democrats in general, and the particularly urgent task of the present moment when interest in politics, and in questions of socialism, has been aroused among the widest sections of the population."

The *Short Course* explains: "Lenin considered that such a newspaper would serve not only to weld the party ideologically but also to unite the local bodies within the party organizationally. The network of agents and correspondents of the newspaper, representing the local organizations, would provide a skeleton around which the party could be built up organizationally."

But Lenin himself went on: "This network of agents will form the skeleton of precisely the organization we need, namely one that is sufficiently large to embrace the whole country, sufficiently wide and many sided to effect a strict and detailed division of labor; sufficiently tried and tempered to be able unswervingly to carry out its own work under all circumstances, at all turns and in all contingencies; sufficiently flexible to be able to avoid open battle against an enemy of overwhelming strength when he has concentrated all his forces at one spot, and yet able to take advantage of the awkwardness of this enemy and to attack him whenever and wherever least expected."

From this we see that Lenin understood propaganda

to be not merely a means of enlisting a following by conversion, or of confusing and weakening the enemy by a
constant bombardment of words, ideas and slogans, but
as the shield and sword of a dynamic group which aimed
at using both of these effects to its own advantage. But
Lenin went even further than that. He divided his party
into two groups. At the center was to be a small, compact
group of a dozen or so experienced revolutionaries, "no
less," as he put it, "professionally trained than the police,"
who were to give their full time to coordinating the secret
as well as the overt functions of the entire organism. The
rest was to be a broad network of organizations. Lenin
wrote: "The centralization of the more secret functions in
an organization of revolutionaries will not diminish, but
rather increase the extent and quality of the activity of a
large number of other organizations which are intended
for a broad public and are therefore as loose and non-secret
as possible such as trade unions, workers' circles for self-
education and the reading of party literature, socialist and
democratic circles among *all* other sections of the population, etc., etc. We must have such circles, trade unions, and
organizations everywhere in as large numbers as possible
and with the widest variety of functions; but it would be
absurd and dangerous to confuse them with the organization of revolutionaries, or to obliterate the border line
between them."

It is worth while to note that this description of a so called
political party, written forty-six years ago, today precisely
describes the Communist party of the United States, Great
Britain or France, and it is just as accurate a description
of the apparatus by which the Soviet Union is governed.

But this should occasion no surprise; all of them were constructed on Lenin's blueprint.

With the centralization of Communist power in Moscow, and the emergence of the Soviet Union as a nation controlled by Communists, Communist propaganda takes on a dual character. In non-Communist countries it is, as it was for Lenin in Russia, the sword and shield of the local Communist armies seeking power. At the same time it is, and unless the cold war turns into a shooting one, will continue to be the favored instrument for promoting the Soviet Union's intention to dominate the world. Whenever and wherever these two aims conflict, the interests of the local party must be subordinated.

Any isolated item of propaganda may be a truth, a half-truth or a monstrous lie, but it is most often a skillful blend of all three. Propaganda is thus not often readily recognized. For sample analyses, I have chosen three examples, originating on three different levels and aimed at three different groups. But it is necessary to lay down a warning at once: These samples do no more than scratch the surface of the infinite variety and skillful techniques the propagandists have developed.

A.

For several years now it has been the custom of nearly every American traveler who manages to breach the Kremlin walls for an interview with Stalin, to ask the great man if he thinks the Soviet Union can live side by side in peace with the capitalist United States. Stalin has always replied that he thinks it is possible. A few have gone a bit further, and asked what conditions would make it possible. To

them Stalin has replied that in his view a return by the
United States to the "principles" of Roosevelt would be
desirable.

Before going into what he means by the "principles of
Roosevelt" let us look at the immediate effect of these
interviews. They are, first of all, blazoned in newspaper
headlines under some such abbreviation as "Stalin Says
Peace Possible." This becomes the guide for all the unthink-
ing people who preface every discussion of the Soviet
Union by the declamation, "I don't want war," to add
"Well, if our State Department would only change its
attitude, we wouldn't have to have war." Or, as more often
happens, they say, "What are our people doing, anyhow,
trying to get us into a new war?" So that our first reaction
to this gambit is a questioning of the motives and behavior
of our own government.

Everybody knows that nobody wants war. But only those
who have spent some time and energy in the study of this
universal cry seem to understand how it is being used in
the propaganda world of today. Not long ago, in Warsaw,
there was a congress of youth. It was one of those Com-
munist-inspired, Communist-controlled gatherings that
seem to be increasing in number and scope. A woman of
Warsaw passed a group of excited young people who were
yammering at each other with loud volubility. The scene
interested her and she stopped, having in mind to ask
them what they were doing. But before she could do that,
one of their number, a tall, unshaven, brusque Greek lad,
pounced on her. "Where do you stand?" he demanded to
know.

"How do you mean?" the woman asked.

"Are you for liberty, or do you represent the bourgeoise?"

"Oh," she said, "I don't think about such things. I have my two children and my husband, so I merely run my house and . . . politics . . . well I really don't. . . ."

"So," the Greek said, "you're a mother?"

"Yes," she said, "and I don't try to think about. . . ."

"But," he pushed, "if you're a mother then you must be against war?"

"Oh," the woman said, "but, of course I'm against war. . . ."

"Ah-h," said the young Greek, "then you must be for us. . . . Long live Markos. . . ."

This sounds silly, I know. But it is an argument that is being used in just so many words not only in Warsaw, or Paris, or London, or Washington but everywhere there are Communists. And, whether we like it or not, as long as we fall for it, as too many of us have been doing for too long, Stalin will continue to use such means to try to weaken us as a nation by dividing us against our own government. For it is the Communist preachment that peoples want peace, and only governments which are in the grip of monopoly capitalists want war. For purposes of appealing to the people of the United States, and inciting them against their own government, Stalin takes the view that President Truman is, today, the puppet of monopoly capital.

This leads us abruptly into the second important phase of these Stalin pronouncements which are so often so widely published in the United States. What, as far as Stalin is concerned, are the "principles of Roosevelt"? Well, Roosevelt took the attitude that Stalin, like most politicians of Roosevelt's experience, would repay in kind the favors extended him. The first principle of Roosevelt's approach was to give Stalin anything he asked for. The giving was not limited to Lend-Lease, and Lend-Lease cannot be evaluated in percentages of total effort or dollar value. Lend-Lease plugged gaps in the Russian war effort which, had they not been plugged, might have made a decisive difference. As Stalin sees it the first Rooseveltian principle was unlimited giving.

At Teheran and Yalta Roosevelt's generosity leaped all international barriers, and he gave Stalin things which were not in his power of gift, such as parts of China. We are told now that this was done to "induce" Stalin into the war against Japan, but Stalin himself must have spent many a genial hour chuckling over the fact that he had been bribed into doing something he most certainly would have done anyway.

Certainly Stalin would like to see a return to the principles of Roosevelt by the United States. But when he speaks of the Rooseveltian principles he means something quite different from what most United States citizens understand. So, by playing on words like peace and principles he adroitly seeks to undermine the authority of the United States government by alienating its people. Our recent election proved how far he has fallen short of success, but it would be imprudent to forget that by constantly mouthing just these Stalinisms Henry Wallace attracted the votes of more than one million people. Stalin's propaganda has not proved to be as big a factor in the United States as he would like it to be, but a million votes is not neglible.

While Stalin continues to play upon the naïve and the

thoughtless in the United States with this line of peace
with capitalism and Rooseveltian principles, the people of
the Soviet Union are being told something quite different.
On April 17, 1946, P. F. Yudin gave a lecture to an audience
of 1,700 persons in the big hall of the Polytechnic Museum
in Moscow. Yudin is an important person in the Soviet
Union. In matters of theory and Marxian interpretation he
is an adviser to the Kremlin and one of the leading figures
of the Lenin School to which Communists from all over the
world go for higher Communist training. It was Yudin, for
example, who was given the job of supervising the newspaper of the Cominform when that new limited version
of the old Communist International, or Comintern, was
established in 1947. Whatever Yudin says can be accepted
as authoritative.

The subject of this lecture was the transition from Socialism to Communism in the Soviet Union. In the course of
it Yudin remarked that, in the United States, production
had already reached the point where Communism could be
instituted immediately, and then he went on: "What is the
state? First and foremost it is the army. The USSR must
have an army stronger than those of all our enemies put
together. The USSR is surrounded by capitalist states
which are constantly sending in streams of diversionists
and spies.

"In capitalist states the army is used for home oppression, that is, it has an introvert function. But in the USSR
the army has a purely extrovert function. As long as there
is capitalist encirclement the army will continue to exist,
even under Communism. Therefore, only when the encir-
cling powers themselves become Communist will the army

become no longer necessary. Just as no army is needed in the relations between the Russian Socialist Federated Soviet Republic and the Ukraine, so no army will be needed in our relations with an English Soviet Republic or a German Soviet Republic."

At the end of this lecture Yudin answered a number of questions, and two of them have special interest for us:

> Q. As technical progress is faster in the United States than in the USSR, does that mean that the United States will attain Communism * before the USSR does?
> (From the audience there were many shouts of "Only after a war.")
>
> Yudin's A. There must first be a revolution. But once the progress starts economic transition to Communism may well be much faster than in the USSR.
>
> Q. Will there ever be Communism in the United States?
> A. Only after the liquidation of the bourgeoisie.
> Q. Will Communism be brought about everywhere by revolutionary means?
> A. Marx maintained that in England and America the dictatorship of the proletariat might be brought about by peaceful means. But Lenin pointed out that this is no longer true, owing to improvements in police methods and control in those countries.

* This question is based on a form of dialectical hairsplitting. The Communist party asserts that the Soviet Union is now a Socialist state but soon will become a Communist one. The difference, say the Communists, is that in a Socialist state each person gets paid according to the value of what he contributes in labor or other service. Under Communism they are to receive what they need. True Communism is thus a present impossibility anywhere and will continue to be one for many generations to come if not for ever. No nation can make enough goods to create such a state. Even at its present unprecedented level of production, the United States could not provide it for one-third its people. Besides, man's appetite for goods and services is limitless. Who is to say what a man's needs are? Will it not be necessary to have police for that purpose just as police are now necessary to make sure no impure thoughts obtrude themselves to obstruct the Communist party state?

The meaning of all this is inescapable. In the Kremlin's view peace between the Soviet Union and the United States will become an absolute certainty only when the United States becomes a Soviet republic. When Stalin talks about the possibility of peace between the Communist party's Soviet Union and the capitalist United States, he not only says something he does not believe, but does it for the purpose of aiding the Communist movement in this country.

B.

Stalin's type of propaganda is aimed at all the people of the United States. For another type of propaganda, aimed at making an impression without necessarily using either newspaper or radio, there is the case of Alexander Kuzminsky.

Kuzminsky was an American citizen of Russian parentage who, during the depression thirties, returned to Russia as a workman. Unlike most Americans who did that, he clung to his American citizenship, even when, at the outbreak of war, he found himself in the Red Army, serving as a private or, as the Russians phrase it, a common soldier. Kuzminsky lost one hand, and most of the fingers on the other, during the fighting. He was demobilized and given the common soldier's disability pension of about 100 roubles a month, which, he soon found, was not enough to keep him alive. He could not return to his old trade, nor had he been taught any other. In spite of the claim that there is no unemployment in the Soviet Union, Kuzminsky became, indubitably, an unemployed man.

One day, ragged, filthy, hungry, Kuzminsky turned up

at the American Embassy in Moscow hoping, as he said, to establish his American citizenship and get help in returning to the United States. His citizenship was quickly proved, but before anything else could be done he had to get Soviet permission to leave the country which, in most cases, proves to be impossible.

However, the American consular officer was a man of imagination. He computed what Kuzminsky would have received had he served the same length of time and received the same injuries in the service of his own country. He then wrote a letter addressed to whomever it might concern in which he stated that Alexander Kuzminsky was an American citizen who had fought for Soviet Russia. The letter went on to say that had he been in the United States Army, Kuzminsky would have received so and so many dollars for life. To the bottom of the letter was affixed a great red seal complete with dangling ribbons, globs of sealing wax and all the other ruffles and flourishes of protocol.

About a month later Kuzminsky came back. He had on a new Red Army uniform, new boots and a new greatcoat. From a demobilized common soldier Kuzminsky had, within the month, been elevated to the rank of captain, with four glistening little silver stars on his shoulder boards to prove it. More than that he had a letter, signed by Stalin himself, in which the Soviet government guaranteed to pay him a monthly pension of 150 United States dollars for life. To top it all, he had an exit visa permitting him to leave the Soviet Union and a guaranty of transportation.

Several times since my return to the United States I have caused efforts to be made to find Kuzminsky at the several

Detroit addresses he left with the United States Embassy in Moscow. These efforts have failed to turn him up. But I know that wherever he is, when he tells the tale of what happened to him in the Soviet Union his listeners are impressed by the generosity and the solicitude Stalin's government has for its people. Of course, very few of them are likely to know that Kuzminsky is the only case of his kind in Soviet history or be able to visualize what sort of shape he was in before the United States consular officer in Moscow gave him that magic letter.

C.

The third item of propaganda is taken from a little book prepared by the National Council of American-Soviet Friendship and published by the Jacques Cattell Press of Lancaster, Pennsylvania, in 1944. The title is *Science in Soviet Russia*.

Now the National Council of American-Soviet Friendship is one sample of what Lenin meant when he said, "We must have such circles, trade unions, and organizations everywhere in as large numbers as possible and with the widest variety of functions. . . ." It draws its inspiration and much of its material from a Soviet organism called the All Union Society for Cultural Relations with Foreign Countries (and known as VOKS) which is an appendage of the Soviet Communist Party Central Committee's Section for Agitation and Propaganda.

While in Moscow, I had a considerable amount of contact with VOKS, and with its chief, a man named Kemenev. I know from experience that the attitude VOKS maintained toward cultural exchange with foreigners in all fields was summed up by Kemenev's answer to a question as to why Ernest Hemingway was not invited to visit the Soviet Union. Kemenev said: "I don't think he likes us enough."

In any event, this little book is evidence of one of the activities of papers read by a number of people at a so-called science panel held by the Council in New York on November 7, 1943. It contains nothing that would be of specific value to any scientist, but much that tends to suggest that Soviet science is wonderful.

In the preface, written by Dr. Walter B. Cannon of Harvard University, we find this statement: "In 1935, when the International Physiological Congress met in Moscow, the International Committee of which I was a member had the privilege of a conference with Molotov in the Kremlin. During a session of about two hours he explained to us the interest of the Soviet government in the advancement of science. . . . It is significant that at that time the expenditure for scientific institutions and research was a larger item in the national budget of the Soviet Union than in the budget of any other civilized country."

I cannot make out just what the earnest Dr. Cannon meant to convey by that statement. Does he want the United Sates government to take over and finance all the scientific institutions and research laboratories in the United States? Remember the Soviet Union has no research laboratories financed by industries, no schools or institutes supported wholly or in part by private endowment, or in fact any scientific enterprise of any sort which is not financed by the state. But whatever Dr. Cannon may have meant to say, what he did imply was that in the Soviet

Union science and scientists are more tenderly and encouragingly cared for than they are elsewhere. Which just isn't so.

Here we have a propaganda item aimed at a special group — scientists. We also have a type of propaganda statement which is true, but which carries a false implication that can only be dispelled by thoughtful analysis, and unfortunately too few of our people are equipped with the necessary knowledge of Soviet reality to make the analysis.

So far, I have dealt with the outflowing forms of Soviet propaganda — that is to say the barrage of words and ideas laid down on the people of the United States which has, as its major intent, the creation of unrest, dissatisfaction and division. But the Soviet people are also under a constant barrage which has the opposite intent of creating unity, political solidity, and an unquestioning attitude toward all acts of government.

According to *Pravda* of May 5, 1947, there are 7,000 newspapers and 360 magazines in the Soviet Union. The newspapers, a good many of which are published twice weekly or weekly, have a total circulation of about 30,000,000 and the magazines altogether print some 6,000,000 copies. In one respect, these figures — if accurate — are remarkable. In the United States, and in Britain, the total circulation of all newspapers is considerably greater than the population total, which means that millions of persons buy more than one newspaper. In the Soviet Union only about one in every six persons buys any newspaper. As for the magazines, the combined circulation of all Soviet publications in this field is nearly equalled by *Life* magazine alone and more than doubled by *The Reader's Digest*.

However, this does not have as strong a bearing on the distribution of information as it might seem to have. Soviet newspapers, while not necessarily identical, are so nearly so that the difference between them is microscopic. *Pravda* is printed from identical matrices in nine cities, and its total circulation accounts for more than one-tenth of the circulation of all newspapers.

From a Soviet newspaper, one gets little more than a glimmer of what is going on in the outside world. Recently, in the *New York Times Sunday Magazine*, the Russian specialist Harry Schwartz compared the *Times* of Nov. 2, 1948, with *Pravda* for the same day.

Here are the headlines the *Times* carried on its first page that day:

1. Mukden is bombed by Nanking planes as Reds capture it.
2. Premier of China offers resignation.
3. Ross death inquiry blocked by Soviet.
4. Bunche says truce rules in Palestine; Israel rebuffs U.N.
5. Forrestal Commands services to take no rows to Congress.
6. Luce suite robbed of $20,000 in gems.
7. 6,000,000 in state expected to vote. [New York State]
8. President advises the people to vote their convictions.
9. Vandenberg bars any cabinet post.
10. Dewey calls issue strong, united U.S.
11. Vote of 50,000,000, record for nation, is expected today.

Eleven front-page stories, each presented without a hint of editorial opinion. The *Times* that day carried 23 pages of news and was a 52-page newspaper.

Pravda had four pages, and two of those were given over to a long essay headlined: "The Struggle for the Victory of Socialist Economics," which made the point that the Soviet system was superior to vampire capitalism, and showed the people of all countries "their inevitable and not distant future."

This point was also emphasized in a page-one, three-column editorial headlined: "Under the banner of Lenin, under the leadership of Stalin, forward to the victory of Communism." The editorial reviewed the slogans issued for the celebration of the October revolution and picked as the most important: "Workers of all countries! Expose the aggressive schemes of the incendiaries of new wars! Rally the forces of democracy in the struggle for lasting peace and the security of peoples."

A story on the Berlin crisis was headed: "The Berlin crisis and the aggressive policies of the Anglo-American Bloc." A survey of the French strike quoted the French Communist Maurice Thorez as saying: "It is completely evident the Western Powers don't want peace with the Soviet Union."

A dispatch from Berlin quoted the German Communist Party as demanding a peace treaty now, and the evacuation of all foreign troops from Germany.

A story from Bucharest told about the trial of an Anglo-American spy ring, composed of traitors and spies in the employ of agents of American and English espionage.

A Paris story depicted the Soviet representative at the United Nations fighting for the rights of oppressed colonial peoples in Africa.

A roundup of United States election news consisted chiefly of Henry Wallace's views on United States policy towards the Soviet Union. Wallace got ten inches of space, Truman five, Dewey none.

Mr. Schwartz commented: "In *Pravda* every sentence, every line, every article aims at some specific goal. The goals vary from stimulating production and exposing delinquents to indoctrinating Soviet citizens with the belief that Russia's leaders are omniscient and their policies wisest and best."

The comparison could be made any day, in any year, and it would be much the same.

Once, in Moscow, I met a Russian-born American woman who had, in some miraculous fashion she did not relate, obtained permission to return to her native village for a visit to her aged parents.

The village was in a terrible plight. Most of its people were really hungry — "hungrier," they told her, "than they had been even in the darkest days of Lenin's civil war" — which she could remember as having been pretty bad. But in these peasant cottages, cans which had once contained American spam and American stew meat were being used for flower vases.

Each peasant cottage had a loud-speaker which was wired to the one radio receiver in the village, and all day long they listened to the plots Radio Moscow was incessantly discovering, all of which suggested that the United States was getting ready to make war on the Communist state.

"It must be true," they told this returned American girl. "It must be true. Look, during the war, the Americans sent us food. Now we are hungrier than ever, and they do not send us food any more. It must be they want to kill us."

The American girl first tried to show why their reasoning

was wrong, and then to show why the radio was wrong. But she made no progress until she lost her temper. Glaring in angry scorn at the poor villagers she asked: "What have you got that any American would want?"

But she did not make them angry. She simply shocked them into thinking for themselves, for once. And as they looked at the good clothes of this *Amerikanka,* and at the rich presents she had brought, and then at their own shabby clothes and cottages, they asked themselves with increasing wonder, "What *have* we got that any American would want?"

There was only one answer and they eventually found it — "Nothing."

But Radio Moscow went right on, as it still does, and will next year, and for many years, repeating headlines from *Pravda.*

INDEX